Loren B. Mead

MORE
THAN
NUMBERS

THE WAYS
CHURCHES
GROW

an alban institute publication

The Publications Program of The Alban Institute is assisted by a grant from Trinity Church, New York City.

Library of Congress Catalog Card Number 92-75724
ISBN 1-56699-109-9

CONTENTS

INTRODUCTION

Years ago I spent a year in a parish near London. When I tried to discover what I would be doing as pastor there, I asked an ordinary—I thought—question: "How many members are there?"

A year later, still unclear about how many members *had* been in that parish, I returned to my American parish with a much more complicated understanding of "numbers."

There were about 7,000 people in the parish, and as parish pastor I was "related" to them, including those in the Catholic parish and the Methodist chapel. In that ecclesiastical system, that was the crowd I was officially supposed to baptize, marry, and bury. Of those, there were about 700 on the electoral roll, who had chosen to have their names put down as voters in parish elections. There were about eighty I could count on if we had something organized to carry out. About 200-220 (some of whose names I never got) were the heart of every worship service. There were at least six spiritual giants I knew about. About 300 were involved in one or another subgroup, and about 1,500 came across the church door at least once in that year.

Ever since that year I have looked on "number of members" as an important but problematic statistic. It does tell you something, and you get in trouble if you don't pay attention to it; but its simplicity hides a lot.

This book is about a larger view of how congregations grow or don't grow.

In Chapter One I try to describe some congregations I've known and the complex ways they lived their lives; the model I use tries to make some order of the complexity. In the second, third, fourth, and fifth chapters I focus on four different ways I think all congregations are

called to growth: in numbers, in maturity of faith, in corporate effectiveness, and in transforming the outside world.

I've scattered tools and questions and ideas through the book in
hopes that congregations will use my ideas as triggers for their imaginations. I am not as interested in your reading the book as I am in your
making your own congregation a growing congregation—in as many
ways as possible.

In writing this book I need to acknowledge some very specific support I have received from four long-time associates who have shaped me
and my ideas more than I can say.

Celia Allison Hahn and I have worked together for more than two
decades. She invented a remarkable communications linkage system that
made our office a crossroads of practical knowledge about congregations. Members of Alban are aware of the outflow: that remarkable
journal now called *Congregations* (formerly *Action Information*) and the
flow of monographs and books (well over 100 now), including several by
her. You may not be as aware of how she also helped us work at making
that knowledge flow "two-way traffic." Many of our articles and books
came in over the transom or by dint of hard persuasion from lay persons,
clergy, and other inhabitants of congregations.

Roy Oswald brought his inquiring Canadian Lutheran self into my
life and Alban's soon after Celia. From the day we flew together to Fort
Campbell to study how army chaplains start new assignments, his curi-
osity and tenacity about learning have constantly led me into new terri-
tory. Where something is going on that we don't understand, I know to
send Roy, if we can find a way to do it. I know he will not back away
from even very scary situations; I also know that when he comes back he
will bring better questions and a kit bag full of new insights. His contri-
bution to understanding and supporting the clergy of the churches is
incalculable. The Clergy Development Institute he leads for Alban is the
one education event I consider most likely to help a good pastor move
toward "better."

Speed Leas practically invented conflict management consultation
in the religious world. His long-time association with me and Alban has
put us in the middle of dozens of the most pain-filled moments any
church can experience. But Speed's gift is not just the guts to go into
those difficult, sweaty-palm situations, but to *believe* in health and work
for it even in the middle of chaos. Nobody has seen more lying and

backstabbing, more selfishness and anger. Yet no one I know has been more willing to be vulnerable to the pain, trusting what God is hoping to do with human sin. Speed's ability to learn from practice and his talent for teaching have enormously increased the number of people around the churches who can help when church fights break out. Few are his equal in knowing the technology of change. His work, and that of the consulting network he invented, will be a major resource to us all in grappling with the incredible diversity facing the churches and society in the next few decades.

Leslie Buhler is the latecomer—she's only been a partner in the enterprise a little over a decade. Entering a religious system from a very different professional field, Leslie's gifts of organization, comprehensive thinking, and caring management were essential to harness the rich chaos of individual gifts in the life of Alban. Watching her I learned a lot about "organic growth" and began to understand why St. Paul listed administration as a spiritual gift. She helped all of us invent our own future and structures adequate to support that vision.

What a privilege to learn from people like this. I've often said it feels like being a plow horse yoked to a bunch of thoroughbreds. They have been my tutors as well as my colleagues.

There are others. So *many* others. People who have asked me questions I couldn't answer. Others who have told me troubles I didn't want to hear. People whose long-ago comment got under my skin, lay dormant for years, then—when I was finally ready to hear—popped up and opened my eyes.

Introductions to books give you a chance to say things like this. I hope you find this book helpful. If you do, please know that the reason I write at all is because people like these push me and prod me, teach me and lead me. They model for me that we must work together and help each other.

Loren B. Mead
Ash Wednesday, 1993

CHAPTER I

How Real Churches Grow, or Don't

Stories of Churches

Churches seem to have personalities. I mean local churches, the ones we sometimes call parishes or congregations.

Each one seems to have its own way of relating to others, its own way of deciding what is important, its own way of making mistakes, and its own way of working out its future. There are often similarities, and research people have noted how congregations of a similar size sometimes share many common characteristics (Rothauge). Others talk about the location of the congregation as having a lot to do with the way they are (Walrath). Others suggest that congregations are shaped by their relationships with their communities (Roozen, McKinney, and Carroll). Still others argue that each congregation has its own distinct culture and history (Hopewell).

There are lots of ways that you can look at congregations. Each characterization or perspective tells you something. It is more common for people to see a congregation as different because of its denominational background (Baptist or Episcopal or Congregational), its theological style (conservative or liberal, liberation or neo-orthodox or evangelical), its ecclesiological style (high church or low church), or its piety (formal and liturgical, informal, or charismatic). The language the researchers use, their more common statements of the differences, or our own words when we tell how we experience a congregation are all ways we try to put into words something that may lie beyond words alone.

None fully catches the uniqueness that concerns me. When you get up close to congregations, as I try to do as often as I can, no two really are identical. Each seems to have its own genius, its own spirit. Indeed, this singularity is reflected in the New Testament, where we are told of the "angels" of the different churches, each of which seems to express a different personality.

Since this book is about how churches grow, and since each congregation is special, I want to begin by telling some old stories of congregations I have known, reflecting on how I have seen them grow. In one sense, I will be describing something of the angel of that congregation, as I have seen it. Any participant in the congregation will know aspects of its life that go far beyond what I have been able to identify. They will know its angel better than I do.

I find that churches do not always grow in conventional ways. To begin to explore growth, then, I begin with stories, not theories. All are about real, if disguised, congregations. And these stories will be the framework for what I say about growth.

The Church of the Apostles

The Church of the Apostles is no more. It was a small congregation that appeared in the early sixties in a city in Tennessee. It was a congregation of Presbyterians who "found" each other, the early members having known each other first through social groups, politics, and school networks. They came to realize that they had a desire to take their religion seriously, build a community that really supported them, and address some glaring problems of their town—racial problems, drug problems, and the like. They also felt that those needs were not being addressed in their regular congregations.

Eighteen families covenanted with each other to try to build just such a faith community. They were prepared to invest themselves fully in the effort, no matter what it took. The early marks of the congregation were powerful and innovative worship, intensely personal encounters with one another, and significant political action in town. Their corporate life was not that of conventional congregations. For example, they initiated a drive to integrate local public schools. Once each year they went away together for a religious retreat in which members opened up the deepest parts of their lives to each other. In those retreats and in other parts of their lives significant healing took place for families and for individuals. They developed their own form of preaching. Each week a group studied the scriptures intensely, then selected the Sunday preacher from among themselves.

They kept Presbytery informed, but were not very active in it, nor did they take an active part in denominational mission efforts. Presbytery did not know quite what to do with them and treated them like an adopted child about whom they were both proud and anxious. Members of the congregation, encouraged by each other, got involved in all kinds of civic action. One ran for school board and was elected. Another was appointed, then elected to the county council. Congregational meetings were long and conflicts were painful, but the group maintained a commitment to consensus decision making. They never had a building, and with their small numbers they continually had to scratch to cover their bills, including the three-quarter-time salary of their pastor. They never added very much to their numbers. At their high point there were twenty-five families and six single people. In the mid-seventies, when I knew them best, it had stopped being much fun. Survival problems loomed large. One of them told me, "I just got tired." On Easter Sunday, 1978, they had a great reunion of all those who had been part of the congregation, celebrated their life, had a big party, and closed the congregation. For many of them, life in that congregation had been a life-changing event. They still talk about it when they meet around town or at parties.

Reflections on Growth

The Church of the Apostles never experienced any significant numerical growth. Indeed, they were a clear failure in the numbers game. But extraordinary things happened to some of the people; many of *them* grew. They gave and received the kind of support and encouragement that helped them become more than they had been before. Those people experienced personal growth. The town benefited, too. People in the congregation made a difference in the life of the community by living out the values and meanings they learned in the congregation. Many members, not just the ones who ran for office, got involved in public life as they never had before. I wonder about the emotional growth that occurred when they decided to close the congregation. Was that growth? And the people who did not stick with the congregation over the years:

What happened to them? Did they became active in other congregations? I wonder how the congregation affected the Presbytery and its other congregations. I wonder what happened to the members of Apostles after the congregation closed. There are lots of unanswered questions about different kinds of growth.

Apostles blew it on numbers, but I have to say I see growth in its story.

First Church Middletown

First Church Middletown has been there forever. It sits on the town green in New England and has always been at the heart of the community. It has been—by the lights of its denomination—a marginal congregation for most of its life. The rural area around it changed little for a century, with only a slow, steady decline of population as the young people grew up and moved off to Boston or Hartford or Portland. The church has stayed solvent because the older members have tremendous pride and commitment and give sacrificially. Occasionally a small bequest sweetens the pot a bit. Over the years several of the young people have gone to seminary and now serve in other parts of the country. When I last spoke to the pastor of First Church and asked how it was going, he said, "Well, I'm holding on. Only five more years to retirement." Each year the congregation is a little smaller and a little grayer.

Reflections on Growth

Decline. You cannot say anything else when you look at what's going on there. A long, slow decline. What can you say about that in terms of growth? What about older people, facing the end of life and the decline of their community? Does the church's presence help them grow in the task of holding steady, in holding on as alternatives diminish? What about the young people—and not just the ones who went to seminary? Did the church help them grow? How does a church grow in the midst of a declining community? Can a church whose future prospects are declining be a growing church? In what sense?

Faith Lutheran Church

Faith Church is in a small town five miles from a much larger university town in Ohio. The luck of the draw brought a dynamic young pastor to Faith Church for her first solo pastorate. She did an absolutely extraordinary job. A very quiet, unchanging congregation was jump-started. The pastor quickly made contact with people at the university nearby, and floods of young people came to hear the exciting preaching and to get involved in workcamps, social programs, and the general vitality this young pastor generated. Lutheran clergy in the university town were not entirely pleased at the decimation of the programs they had planned. Faith Church's older members were bewildered by what happened, thrilled with the packed Sunday services, but unsure about the different kind of music and the way the parish hall was being used. First thing anybody knew, the pastor was called to a university chaplaincy in Nebraska. With strong help from the bishop, the congregation called a new pastor, one cast more in the mold of their past experience. Things returned to "normal." There is not a lot at Faith Church now to attract the university students, but the older members find a church experience that fits them better.

Reflections on Growth

How is "growth" in numbers related to the charisma of the leader? Was this growth healthy? How do we make sense of this temporary burst of growth in members and activity? Is the cessation of the growth a good thing or a bad thing? How can you know? Should the bishop have taken a stronger role? Was it a good idea to pull that pastor out of Faith Church and put her in a university chaplaincy? What kind of growth was there for Faith's regular members?

Trinity Church

Trinity is an old colonial church in tidewater Virginia. Almost nobody ever moves to town and nobody moves away except the young people after their schooling. Trinity Church has always had about 100 members,

fluctuating up or down by ten or so from decade to decade. Clergy come
and go, but they don't make a lot of difference. Richmond, Norfolk, and
Charlottesville each have a half-dozen leading citizens who grew up and
went to Sunday School under Miss Marie, an extraordinary lay person
who ran the school with an iron hand for two generations and just died a
few years ago. Miss Marie's niece has been a parish leader for years and
is responsible for one of the finest adult Bible study classes in the state.
Trinity has a Thanksgiving and Christmas baskets-for-the-poor program
and takes much pride in always paying its share of the denominational
mission giving. Its members tend to be very conservative pillars of the
local establishment. Nothing much changes around there, and that is fine
with most people.

Reflections on Growth

Stability, rather than change or growth, seems to be the watchword at
Trinity. There does seem to be a strong value of education in the faith.
But there seems to be no feel of numbers as particularly important. One
wonders what the church communicates about what it means to be part
of the establishment and what is expected of one who is in such a role.
What does it mean to "grow" in a declining rural environment?

St. Andrew's United Methodist Church

St. Andrew's UMC is just down the street from the Disciples' Church, a
block up from the Presbyterian Church, and three blocks over from the
new sanctuary the Baptists built three years ago. All are in a county seat
in southern Kentucky where approximately eighty percent of the people
are affiliated with one church or another. The cabinet has just appointed
an energetic go-getter to pastor St. Andrew's, hoping it can become fully
self-supporting in the next three years. St. Andrew's has announced a
very ambitious evangelism program in the local newspaper and has se-
cured a commitment from Oral Roberts' righthand man to supervise a
six-month intensive member recruitment drive. The Disciples' pastor
gives me a call. "What's this all about, Loren? The only place he's going to get new members is from me, the Baptists, or the Presbyterians.

We've got a fight going on in our congregation, as you know, and this feels like it will undercut our work. I'm all for evangelism, but this doesn't feel right to me. It feels like sheep stealing."

Reflections on Growth

What does growth mean to the United Methodist Church and pastor? What does it mean to the Disciples' pastor? How do the denomination's needs and strategies impact the local needs? What is the responsibility of the board of St. Andrew's to care about what is going on in the Disciples congregation? What is good in St. Andrew's effort? What may be questionable? What does numerical growth mean in heavily churched areas? Is it the same thing as in areas with a majority of unchurched people?

Second Baptist Church

Second Baptist has been in the same location for decades, just outside the old center of town in southern Minnesota. It has a long history of great preaching and ministry, but things have been slow the past six or eight years. The pastor told me a couple of years ago, "It looks as if the Lutherans are going to take over!" Right after that conversation, however, Honeywell announced that they were building a new plant right on the edge of Second Baptist's "turf." Since then things have gone crazy. Real estate costs have zoomed. New houses and new businesses are popping up all over. The whole center of action is shifting toward Second Baptist. Imaginative work at Second Baptist has increased membership from 300 to 390 in just two years. Projections suggest that the church could double in size in the next five years. The board and the trustees are at their wit's end. Should they start a building program now or wait a year until the old mortgage is paid up? What do they do for parking? Where do they put the children in the meantime? Where do they get the energy to do all they must do to manage all the new challenges and not let the traditional strengths get lost? How do they care for the old members while flooded with the needs of the new? Is the old pastor up to the new challenge? What do they need to do about enlarging the staff? When?

Reflections on Growth

What's the difference between "circumstantial" growth and commitment to growth, between "windfall" growth and planned growth? Does it matter? How does one understand one's responsibility for the new persons as "stewardship?" How do you manage chaotic growth? How do you see that the other needs generated by growth, e.g., Christian education, shepherding, and sheer administration, are cared for? What new kinds of care do the oldtimers require? What new demands are there to assimilate this flood of newcomers? What other kinds of growth are needed?

St. Anthony's Catholic Church

St. Anthony's is near downtown Milwaukee and has long been "home" to a community whose roots remain close to eastern Europe. Several members of St. Anthony's became aware of the incredible suffering in the local gay community because of AIDS and brought this to the attention of their deacon, then to the parish staff. A small, but very significant ministry developed. Support groups were established, meals were provided for those who could not manage their own care, and the resources of a hospice were brought to bear. This quiet ministry of caring attracted the attention of Catholics and many others in the Milwaukee area and some of them began worshipping at St. Anthony's. Anxiety about AIDS and uncertainty about homosexuality became profound problems, however, for many of St. Anthony's traditional members. Income and attendance slipped significantly. Parish leaders struggle with what to do. The money and attendance problems have been enough to attract the attention of the diocese.

Reflections on Growth

What does growth mean in this story? Some people obviously are identifying an area of terrible human pain and seeking to grow in ministry to that pain. Others find this ministry a barrier and problem. Where is growth in this story? What growth is called for? What can the leaders be or do that responds to the opportunity?

St. Martin's Catholic Church

St. Martin's is a small outpost of the Catholic Church, located in rural Missouri, with a priest who commutes two days a week. Four years ago a parishioner came in to unburden herself. To this day she is not sure why she went there then; it was just a life-long, shameful secret that she had to share. In short, it was a case of sexual abuse over the years by the uncle who had lived in their home while she was growing up. Her own horror and shame had blocked the experience from her memory for years, but when all of it surfaced, she needed help. The priest listened and listened and listened. (Later he told me, "I honestly did not know what to say, so I did what God apparently wanted me to do—I shut up and listened!") What was remarkable was that as she grew more able to share her pain the parish slowly began to listen, too. Other parish members brought their own pain forward, and as they did, they began to hear a call. The result? Other congregations joined the dialogue and a community program was set up to help people deal with the results of sexual or other abuse and to work at the preventative end as well.

Reflections on Growth

I do not know the numbers related to this story. My hunch is that there aren't many numbers to know. The town is small and rural. Not many people join churches or leave churches in towns like that. And I am not sure how to describe the growth I do see there. But it feels to me that a kind of growth has occurred—growth in understanding human pain and trying to care for its victims.

Third Presbyterian Church

Third Presbyterian is in what used to be the outskirts of Seattle after the Second World War. It became a pretty traditional Presbyterian church—white-collar professionals were its core. A succession of capable pastors spent a few years there enroute to high-steeple ministries, and congregational leaders took pride in doing everything by the book—decently and in order! Three years ago a small group including some leaders of the session attended a renewal retreat in Portland. They were greatly taken with the gifts of the retreat leader. A few months later when a pastoral vacancy occurred, it developed that this charismatic leader was chosen to be the new pastor. The new pastor is installing a new style of life in the congregation, marked by high-commitment membership standards, renewal retreats and lay-witness weekends, prayer and praise meetings, and a new style of preaching ("Bible thumping and holy rolling" as described by a disgruntled older member; "Gospel preaching" as described by a newer member). There was a radical change in worship and in the way session meetings were held. The new pastor assumed a dominant leadership role to which many members were opposed, feeling that it violated their understanding of Presbyterian polity and their own traditions. A serious split has begun to occur. Several of the older members are talking about leaving. Presbytery is getting worried about what the rumor mill says. A strong group in the congregation is excited about the new direction and strongly supports the pastor. That group is actively recruiting new members, both from outside the congregation and from the "conservatives" in the congregation.

Reflections on Growth

Several kinds of growth seem involved here. There is a sense of growth in at least a subgroup in the congregation of an intense, intentional kind of commitment, and there are beginning signs of some people being attracted to that concept. But there is the problem of a congregational split and the relationship of this new life with the past life and identity of the congregation. Is this growth healthy or unhealthy? Says who? Why, or why not?

Stony Valley Church

Once a strong congregation in a working-class area of Detroit, Stony Valley Church has kept itself together and maintained its morale, even though many of its members have moved away and the area has been hit with terrible unemployment. The church is only able to pay for a half-time pastor, ordained a Baptist, for this Disciples congregation. The congregation has made fitful but sincere attempts to reach out to an African-American population to the east of the parish buildings. Three African-American families have joined the eighty other families that make up the congregation. A small bequest three years ago (one that produces about $3,500 a year) led the congregation to struggle about what they most needed to do. Ideas were so different (fix the boiler, increase the time of the pastor, set up a feeding program for the hungry, revamp the education program, etc.) that the congregation got involved in a serious study of itself and the community.

One fact that seemed to capture people's imaginations was that there were simply no resources in the area to help people figure out how to get a job. So a small beginning has been made by renting space in a shopping center, brokering services from public agencies and a nearby university to help neighborhood people analyze their own skills, locating training opportunities, and getting some help seeking work. The congregation's decision was not primarily shaped by jobs and money, but by a concern that people discover their gifts and learn how to use those gifts in service to the community. So while the community sees a job center, the congregation sees it as a place for people to discover their ministries in the world. So far there has been no impact on membership of the congregation, although a number of neighborhood groups and agencies now relate to the congregation.

Reflections on Growth

The growth I see here is in the realm of ideas. This congregation came up with a really different way of seeing what it might be called on for a ministry. The jury is out on whether they can maintain this ministry, or on what may happen to it as a result. Who can know about either? Would a different disposition of the bequest have given more measurable results?

Where Do These Stories Point?

Each of these stories is about something unique. Each describes a special group of people, motivated by their own sense of what God calls them to be and do, sitting in a special community of social and economic realities, living with its own story, filled with individuals and groups that do not exist anywhere else. None of these stories describe anything spectacular. One can see in every one of them something winsome and appealing, but one might also see something that may not feel right.

My thesis is that each of these stories gives a few clues about how congregations are called to grow and how they respond to the call. Every other congregation has its own story to tell. So we must be modest in what we say—God has many more stories that we can ever know, and God knows each of them more deeply even than those who live the stories out.

This book is grounded in these stories, and the stories of the other congregations with which I have worked for four decades. But the reality of God's call for the church to grow is much, much larger than can be discovered here. We deal with clues and seek directions from them: the full reality of God's call to the church is known only in the fullness of all the stories and, therefore, only in the heart of God.

One Scheme for Seeking Our Own Call to Growth

Many years ago a young archdeacon of the Anglican Church of New Zealand was struggling to figure out how to develop new congregations for the burgeoning residential areas around Auckland after the Second World War. He wrote a small book about the experience, *The House Alongside* (Anglican Diocese of Auckland, 1978). He noted that some of the communities he developed grew and some did not. But then he noted that he could identify four different kinds of growth.

I want to share Ted Buckle's model with you, but I want to do so fully understanding that no scheme can exhaust the richness of what is already going on in congregations all across the world. Most of this book will be a way of turning his concept into a method that congregations can use today to analyze their own gifts and seek those aspects of growth that best fit who and where they are.

Buckle suggested that there are four different categories of church growth:

Numerical growth—This is growth in the ways we ordinarily describe it: Sunday attendance, size of budget, and numbers of activities, primarily growth in numbers of active members;

Maturational growth—This growth is in stature and maturity of each member, growth in faith and in the ability to nurture and be nurtured;

Organic growth—This is growth of the congregation as a functioning community, able to maintain itself as a living organism, an institution that can engage the other institutions of society;

Incarnational growth—This is growth in the ability to take the meanings and values of the faith-story and make them real in the world and society outside the congregation. The congregation grows in its ability to enflesh in the community what the faith is all about.

These four modes of growth form the framework of the following chapters. They are also the framework of an invitation to discover and make the most of the call of God to your congregation.

CHAPTER II

Numerical Growth

Numbers in Churches

It should be clear from the thumbnail sketches in the previous chapter that there is much more to church growth than numbers of members. The character of the community, the relationship between the congregation and its community, the nature of the congregation's understanding of its primary mission—all these and more are a part of what we mean by growth.

Be that as it may, in this chapter we want to focus on numbers. Just numbers.

Even that is not easy. When I ask a church leader about the number of members in the congregation, I am usually greeted by a pained look: "Do you mean 'active' or 'on the mailing list' members?" I am asked. Or "Do you mean 'on the rolls' or 'pledgers'?" It seems that the definition changes from year to year and from place to place. Kirk Hadaway has even coined a marvelous name for yet another set of numbers. He refers to those people who will tell the census or the funeral home or the hospital, "I am a Methodist (or whatever)" but do not actually have any organizational contact with the United Methodist Church anywhere. He calls them "Mental Members."

Research tells us that there are a lot of people in this category, one way or another. Institutional loyalists tend to look down on these people as a little lower than apostates, but my experience leads me in another direction. I have found many such people to be hanging onto important meanings by keeping this link to a dormant religious practice. In some cases it represents sets of powerful, long ago experiences or ties to people who, once recalled or brought to the surface by crisis, can help these loosely connected people come "home." The people often experience coming back to church as a real homecoming after a long journey. Many young adults, for example, hold strong, positive, emotional connections to a pastor or a church or a youth experience, even though for many years they may not act on those connections. Often it is those deep things that may be touched when they participate in their own or a friend's wedding, when they go to a funeral, or when they participate in a birth or baptism.

Others, unfortunately, use this mental membership as a protection against involvement. The use of the name of a church innoculates them against looking more deeply at religious experience. It would be convenient if we could tell the one kind of mental member from the other. In the meantime, my case is to treat them with hope and not with contempt.

One thing we do know (and this one makes me wonder who deserves the contempt!) is that lists of congregational members generally get sharply pared whenever a per capita assessment system is installed. We also know that many new pastors take out the shears to "clean up the membership list" as one of the first acts of taking over leadership of a congregation. Again, I know myself well enough to know that there is a little secret place inside each member of the clergy that wants to prove our predecessor cooked the books! It is also true that a long-term pastor tends to leave on the rolls people she or he remembers and doesn't want to drop, even though the last time that person was within the church walls was a decade ago. A kind of sentimental hope lingers there, side by side with an unwillingness to admit a failure of ministry.

Accurate numbers are hard to come by. Dean Hoge, Francis Scheets, and David Roozen discovered that fact when they tried to get accurate information about expenditures in church budgets (*Patterns of Parish Leadership,* Paulist Press, 1988). They discovered that they had to sit down with parish treasurers and pastors and inquire about what each number meant in the parish budget on a line-by-line basis. A similar line-by-line analysis of church membership lists might produce very different statistics than those we now have.

In spite of all this uncertainty about numbers, there are some bottom-line things that need to be said:

— any human institution that does not develop an effective method of recruiting new membership (and leadership) will die. There are no exceptions; and

— any local church that does not care about bringing "outsiders" into a relationship with its faith and its Founder is ignoring a clear imperative of the New Testament.

So, on the basis of sheer survival, as well as scriptural imperative, every congregation must develop a strategy to acquire new members.

Looking at Membership Numbers Systematically

McKinney and Roof (see their chapter "The Demography of Religious Change" in *American Mainline Religion,* Rutgers Press, 1987) present a simple diagram that helps us understand the basic dynamics of changing membership numbers in a denomination or a congregation. The concepts are probably more helpful in dealing with numbers on the scale of a denomination or a region, but the dynamics they describe can be applied at the congregational level too. In this chapter I will also provide tools to help congregations explore these concepts on their own turf.

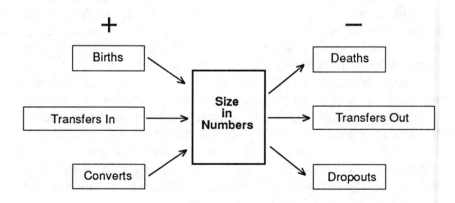

   The dynamics of church membership numbers are quite simple at this level, nothing more than sheer addition and subtraction. The center box represents the membership of the congregation (or other entity) at any particular time. The three forces named on the left describe the ways that membership can be increased. One has only to add up all the entries to know the total additions. The three forces on the right indicate how membership decreases. Again, one has only to add up all the entries to know the total subtractions. Take some baseline total number of members, perform the necessary operations for the desired period of time, and you have a sense of what has happened to membership.

   Let us look, however, at the interaction of the pairs of factors, then at the individual factors themselves. Doing so, I believe, can give us some help in knowing how a congregation might respond to simple numbers with informed action. As we look at these factors, I will also provide worksheets to help you work out their implications in your own situation.

Looking at Paired Factors

Birth and Death

These two factors are the most elemental. The balance between them leads to increases of membership during baby booms and decreases during times of widespread illness and mortality. Other factors can be influential, e.g., a religious group's position on birth control, a discovery of how to preserve life or conquer a terrible illness, the outbreak of a virulent epidemic (in AIDS we are at the front end of one of those factors that could have a major impact on numbers of all kinds in all kinds of institutions—the bubonic plague is supposed to have wiped out one-third to one-half the population of Europe in its day). The balance of these factors is something over which congregations have almost no control. A wise congregation, however, will analyze the balance in its own life in order to plan and to make informed choices.

   First Church, Middletown, tends to have a higher death rate than birth rate, and that looks like a permanent trend. Trinity Church appears to have a similar situation. It is not clear, yet, but Second Baptist Church may be facing a sudden influx of couples of child-bearing age. Paying attention to these balances can help the pastor and the leaders build the appropriate future ministry of the congregation. If Second Baptist's influx is couples of childbearing age, it will mean one thing to the building committee; if it is an influx of pre-retirement couples, it will mean something quite different.

WORKSHEET #1

Birth and Death

Parish births in 24 months ____   Parish deaths in 24 months ____

Baptisms/Dedications (24) ____   Funerals we "staffed" (24) ____

Number infants (3 & under)   Number infants in congregation
on nursery roll ____   not on nursery roll ____

Other factors to consider:

Incapacitating illnesses in last 24 months ____

Number newly confined at home in last 24 months ____

Number entering nursing home care in 24 months ____

Number marriages with couple residing locally ____

Number couples of child-bearing age moved into ____
congregation in past 24 months

Discussion:

1. What in this data is a surprise?

2. What trends appear that need attention?

3. What are we overlooking in our ministry?

4. Is the birth or death rate in the community or in other
   congregations like ours or different?

5. What are the five-year implications for us?

6. What are the ten-year implications?

7. What do we need to change in our record keeping to give us easier
   access to information like this?

* * * * *

Transfers in and Transfers Out

Keeping an eye on this balance is useful, although it may tell more about the transiency of the community than the effectiveness of the congregation. Congregations with high rates of both kinds of transfers may need to think of themselves as training grounds for membership in other congregations! Such congregations are found in some suburbs related to high-turnover industry or congregations in university settings. Such congregations may need to keep an eye on the trends affecting the institutions from which their members are drawn (Is the state cutting back on plans for the university? Is the telecommunications revolution going to make your next door computer plant obsolete?)

High-transfer congregations also make a great demand on the people who stay. It is often overlooked that where many are coming and many leaving, the stable core needs special care and support. I once served in a congregation that had sixty-two percent turnover in one twelve-month period. What I tended to lose sight of in the exciting but chaotic turmoil was that about twenty-five percent of the people stayed decade after decade and gave inordinate service as leaders, training and retraining new members year after year. Roy Oswald of our staff did studies several years ago that described some of these dynamics in the obviously exaggerated situation of a parish in a resort setting (*Resort Ministries*, The Alban Institute).

Second Baptist is experiencing a rapid increase in its inflow of people. It will be important for them to distinguish what percentage comes from church shoppers settling down in a new community, from converts from nonreligious backgrounds, or Baptists moving to town. Faith Lutheran, on the other hand, experienced a kind of hothouse infusion of new members from the university related to a charismatic pastoral leader, with the new members disappearing when the pastor left. That temporary blip in the balance between transfers in and out will not be growth to count on. St. Anthony's experience, on the other hand, is troubling. The transfers out of the traditional members with families from Eastern Europe may become a serious problem, even though it may be caused by an effort to minister to AIDS victims. The priest and the parish leaders need to pay attention.

WORKSHEET #2

Transfers

Transfers in in l2 months ___   Transfers out in l2 months ___

Of those, how many from   Of those, how many to local
local churches ___   churches ___

Of those, how many are   Of those, how many were
pledgers now ___   pledging members ___

Discussion:

1. Are there trends here that need further study (do we need, for example, to check previous years or longer periods of time?)

2. Do we know why the transfers in came, especially the local ones?

3. Do we know why the transfers out left, especially the local ones?

4. To what groups in the congregation do the transfers in belong? Do we need to help them connect?

5. To what groups in the congregation did the transfers out be long? Do we need to troubleshoot those groups? Or help them find new members?

6. Do we know what happened to the ones who left?

7. Do we know what happened to those who left temporarily (to schools, to temporary job assignments)?

8. Do we need to do anything to our information system to keep track of these changes?

* * * * *

Converts and Dropouts

This balance is hard to track. Although a congregation tends to be aware of the arrival of a convert, the process of dropping out is often quiet and unobtrusive. The dropout may have departed several years before the congregation recognizes it. John Savage's classic study of dropouts and what to do about them is dated but still timely. (*The Apathetic and Bored Church Member*, Lead Consultants, 1976).

     Of the congregations I described above, only two—St. Andrew's UMC and Third Presbyterian—are obviously related to this pair of factors in a significant way. At St. Andrew's I think the pastor and leaders are hoping that their campaign brings in converts, or at least disaffected persons; but the Disciples' pastor who phoned me had a different impression. He may have been particularly sensitive because of the conflict in his own congregation. He felt that St. Andrew's was fishing in the troubled waters of "his" congregation in hopes of scooping up a few live ones they could call "converts." Clergy are not above such rationalization!

     The dynamics inside Third Presbyterian may relate to these two factors as well. The rationale for the kind of change instituted by the pastor is often to attract the nonbeliever to a more "genuine" version of the faith. The pastor and the parish leaders need to examine what really happens. In many such situations the actual experience is that *marginal* members of other congregations are attracted, not "unbelievers." Because such changes often lead to loss of some members, careful attention needs to be given to what happens to those who do choose to leave. Do they become dropouts or do they move to different congregations?

WORKSHEET # 3

Converts and Dropouts

Number of members admitted
in past year on adult faith
confession ___

Number adults newly listed
inactive in past 12 months ___

Discussion:

1. Any surprises?

2. What has happened to each of the new members?

   Interview some or all new members to get a biography of their
   membership (see Oswald and Leas, *The Inviting Church,*
   p.100ff for method).

3. What has happened to the newly inactive persons?

   (Who knows them? Where are they? What do we know or need
   to know about why they are inactive?)

Further research possibility:

l. Look at pledge records of five years ago. Determine which of
   those pledgers is no longer active. Find out who has moved
   away and who are still in the community.

2. Do limited exit interviews, carefully and professionally respecting
   privacy.

3. List those who have left the congregation in the past five years because of school graduations, job changes, marriages, *etc.* Find out
   where they are and their current relationship to a church.

* * * * *

Looking at the Factors One by One:
Program and Planning Concerns

Births

Congregations can do little about the birth rate of their members, although it is clear statistically that overall church growth or decline is heavily influenced by the birth rate of the people of a denomination. Some say that birth rate is the most important factor in a denomination's growth. Denominations themselves have not been particularly wise in understanding that fact.

Across our society it has been demonstrated that denominations that move "up" the socioeconomic ladder tend to have lower birth rates and lower member growth rates. For many of the mainline Protestant denominations that have experienced severe member losses over the past few decades, the fact of lower birth rate is an important, often unacknowledged, factor. The high anxiety in those denominations about membership loss often leads to scapegoating (of the "liberals" or the "fundamentalists" or the "clergy" or the "bureaucrats"). Anxiety about member loss may be expected in any denomination whose members move "higher" socioeconomically, with consequent irrational behavior. The turmoil among Southern Baptist churches as the moderates and conservatives do battle may be as much sparked by slowed growth (blue-collar Baptists of a generation ago have become white-collar Baptists with lower birth rates today) as by theological orthodoxies. Blaming the moderates for theological liberalism or the conservatives for fundamentalism as the single cause of membership loss may miss the mark considerably. It makes for good fights but poor membership strategy.

Such anxiety from the denomination can also lead to program planning on the basis of skewed information or emotional assumptions ("The only churches that grow are the conservative ones!" or "The only way to grow is to accept the social mission of the Gospel more stringently.") Pressure for national or regional church growth programs often comes with a mix of this anxiety about institutional survival ("We will double our membership in this decade!"). Concern for numbers is not irrational, but it can lead to an anxiety that does lead to irrational pressures and programs.

To be honest about it, all the research suggests that if people of a congregation or denomination simply had more children there would be a greater likelihood of increasing membership. With tongue only halfway in cheek, I say that a program of *this* kind of membership growth might involve a lot of problems, but it certainly would give an interesting slant to sermons, make for parish evangelism retreats that were a lot more fun, and might even increase church attendance!

Birthrate issues are critical in church growth. Congregations need to keep a sharp eye on their own situations and not get caught up in denominational hysteria. It is also true that congregations need to be primarily reactive—they cannot do much about it, but they had better be prepared for whatever happens.

WORKSHEET #4

Birth Ministry

1. How effective and thorough is our congregation's ministry in preparation for marriage?

2. Do we have ways to identify persons in the congregation who are expecting children? In the community?

3. Do we have (or need to develop) prenatal ministries?

4. What is the state of our facilities for care of the newborn? Our nursery? Its staffing?

5. What is the state of the ministry we provide to parents and sponsors at baptism or dedication? Is there any follow-up?

6. Should we think about preschool or kindergarten programs or expansion of what we have?

7. Is there anything we ought to be doing differently? Who should be involved?

* * * * *

Transfers In

There are three basic kinds of transfers in: People who just appear, take their place, and do nothing official to mark the event, people who have been members of congregations somewhere else and transfered letters or statements of membership to the official files of the new congregation, and people who go through a membership class and formal entry process (sometimes involving a service of confirmation).

Much of the literature on new member ministries focuses on these people (cf. Alban's videotapes *Making Your Church More Inviting* and *Assimilating New Members*). Some general points need to be made:

— people who just show up some Sunday at church may be ready to make commitments, but may also be in what may be a fairly long process of "looking around." How they are treated may either bring them in quickly or assist them on their journey. Effective ministry is important even if there is no immediate payoff in a new member for your congregation;

— many newcomers get overlooked;

— congregational life needs to be examined to see where the entry doors are, the physical and emotional places where a stranger can "get in"; these doors need to be multiplied and well-maintained;

— it takes careful processes, some of which may feel mechanical, to be sure such people are cared for and received;

— the congregation's natural "gate-keepers" need to be identified, affirmed, and deployed;

— training for membership should have a high priority;

— some kind of formal activity of making a commitment and being visibly welcomed into membership seems to help newcomers make an effective connection;

— new members need opportunities to review the meaning of membership at some time after making their initial commitment, and, if appropriate, to make adjustments of expectations; and

— new members need to be connected to groups and people quickly.

WORKSHEET #5

Newcomer Ministry

1. Do we have a system for identifying newcomers and keeping a
    list of them? What is that system? Who is in charge of it?

2. Describe what will happen next Sunday to a person who appears
    at the door as a newcomer. Is there anything that needs changing?

3. Do we have a system for following up? Who is in charge?

4. What are our standards for what it means to belong to this congrega-
    tion, and how do we communicate them to new members?

5. What is our system for getting newcomers connected to those areas in
    which they have an interest?

6. What process do we need to help newcomers rethink, revise, and
    recommit themselves to deeper membership periodically after their
    initial commitment?

7. What do we need to do to rethink what we do in these areas?

* * * * *

Converts

In past generations a number of factors in society have tended to point people toward religious institutions even if they did not belong to or know much about them. Society itself—through public schools, community life, and the give and take of the world—communicated a lot of the stories of faith and a lot of information about the Church, and it even nudged people toward religious life. Those peripheral influences and subtle nudges are less and less a part of the social fabric in today's world. Dean Hoge, using a phrase coined by Peter Berger, says that all those influences compose the "structures of plausibility" for the religious enterprise, and that they have been dramatically lowered in our time. That being the case, we can expect fewer "converts" to come in out of the blue. Some will always be struck as Paul was on the way to Damascus, and we must be readier than Ananias was when that time comes. But the fact is that congregations of the next generation will need to develop skills and sensitivities that have lain fallow in many of them. They will need to rediscover the ability to present the case for faith to those who are total strangers to the biblical story. They will have to learn to receive and nurture people converted from radical unfaith to faith.

We need to be conscious that even our "transfers in" category may include people who are virtual strangers to faith or religion. In our new member classes we may find persons with a technical membership in another congregation who really are illiterate in the faith and have no firsthand experience of commitment. Not much can be taken for granted.

Leaders of membership classes will need to develop higher sensitivity to the needs of different new members. Some will simply be seeking orientation to a denomination's special traditions. Others will be looking for very basic introduction to the dynamics of faith itself and the meaning of the Gospel. Members of the congregation will need more adequate training to be able to articulate their own faith.

WORKSHEET #6

Conversion Ministries

1. What activities of our congregation (or use of our buildings) most often touch people who are likely to be unchurched?

   (Take each such activity and analyze what can be done, by whom, to make an appropriate intervention/invitation to faith.)

2. Who in our congregation seems gifted in reaching unchurched people? How can we affirm their ministries and support them?

3. In what ways can we raise the awareness of members of the congregation of their unchurched neighbors, colleagues, etc.?

* * * * *

Deaths

In dealing with the three factors above, our concern has been how to increase the inflow to the congregation. As we move to the three factors of loss of membership, our concern will be to develop ministry that takes the losses seriously, does what can be done to minimize those losses, but at the same time strengthens the positive ministry of the congregation to its people and the community.

Nothing is certain but death and taxes. There is very little a congregation can do about death or the death rate. On the whole many American denominations and congregations are aging. Such aging will mean a higher part of the membership loss is attributable to death.

In the meantime, however, it is important for the churches to realize the opportunity presented by the presence of the older generation. Those over seventy represent the fastest growing generation in the country. That generation includes more imaginative, healthy, and productive people than the world has ever known before at that age.

Acknowledging the reality of death should not lead churches to overlook the enormous challenge to ministry—and resources for ministry—represented by this "new wave" of population. The possibilities are large. This age group can produce trainers in the faith the way it already has produced volunteers for Meals on Wheels. This group may open doors to elderly persons who have never been exposed to an invitation to faith. Seniors are likely to provide mentors and guides for younger leaders still mired in child care. They may provide a generation who will learn new dimensions of spiritual development and become spiritual directors for the young. They can provide skilled and compassionate ministries of pastoral care in the congregation and in the community.

We can do a lot about optimizing the gifts of a growing aging population. And simply in terms of numbers, our congregations will have more older members, for a lot longer, than ever before in history.

WORKSHEET #7

Ministries with Aging and with Dying

(Note: This may also be used with Chapter 3.)

1. What programs and resources are available in our community to persons of retirement age? Are there gaps? Who should fill those gaps?

2. What serious opportunities are available in our congregation for advanced biblical or theological studies?

3. What is the shape of our congregation's ministry at times of death and bereavement? To families? To friends/associates? To the community of the retired?

4. What opportunities can we create to place older members in teaching, counseling, or leadership roles with younger people of the congregation or community?

5. Check data on Worksheet #1 (Birth and Death) for the number of deaths and the number of funerals. Is there a discrepancy? Is there anything to be done about it?

6. What is the quality of what we are able to do in grief counseling and bereavement ministries?

* * * * *

Transfers Out

Most people transfer out because they have to move to another place. Some people transfer out because of disappointments about the congregation they joined, and some because they never really made connections. The disappointments may be trivial, but they can also be deep and hurtful. None is unimportant. Two specific strategies stand out—one is preventative, the other can help the congregation improve its act.

In all human encounters that matter, people come together with expectations. When expectations are not met exactly, the gap between expectation and reality can cause unpleasant feelings. In congregations these expectations can be magnified by religious and other dimensions. Because of this, we encourage every congregation that accepts people into membership (through transfers, confirmation, or conversion) to expect new members to experience some disappointments and to have a plan on hand to go beyond them. We urge periodic opportunities for all members, but especially new ones, to review and rethink what membership means. A year or two after becoming members, people need a chance—whether corporately or individually—to review what membership has meant, to identify where it has exceeded expectations and where they have been disappointed, less to confess feelings of resentment than to begin to build more realistic expectations for the future. To provide these regular times of reevaluation is likely to reduce the build up of disappointment that can lead to unhealthy leavetaking.

Where reevaluation is done early enough, it can also help locate those members who simply have not been able to connect.

Where possible, someone in the congregation should interview anyone who transfers out. The purpose is two-fold. First, the congregation stands to learn a lot by asking leavetakers about their membership experience. In some cases the congregation will learn about things they will want to change. In other cases those left behind may learn about parts of their lives of which they were unaware. Exit interviews like these can give a congregation many clues to developing a stronger community life. In a few cases, sensitively done exit interviews can lead to the member's deciding to try again. The interviewer should resist trying to become a "sales" person, however, resisting any orientation other than learning from the leavetaker.

Second, the other side of exit interviews is to help the leavetaker and the congregation say "goodbye" to each other. Those leaving will be more able to participate well in a new congregation if they have been allowed and invited to let go of the old one. The letting-go may have some tears as well as some joy. At least one congregation we know requires that the exit interview be done as a public "goodbye" in the midst of worship.

Ministry to Transfers Out

1. Who has transferred out of our congregation in the past year? Get a list of their names. Where are they now? How many are "lost"?

2. Can we still conduct exit interviews with any of them? Is there a way (writing? telephone?) to say goodbye and help them make a new connection?

3. How can we develop a regular process of exit interviewing that is routine for leavetakers?

4. Who formally joined our congregation last year? Get a list of their names.

5. What kind of process can we establish to help those persons rethink what membership means? Where should the responsibility be lodged?

* * * * *

Dropouts

The reality of the dropout phenomenon is dramatic. McKinney and Roof state that the fastest growing religious group in this country is the one that, when asked their denominational preference, checks "No Religious Preference." The clear implication of studies of mainline denominations is that their primary membership loss has been through dropouts, not transfers to another denomination.

Researchers unanimously conclude that dropouts are very hard to reclaim. If you want to reduce the loss to the churches because of dropouts, energy is better spent in prevention than in pursuing those who have left.

Research by Dean Hoge, Benton Johnson, and Donald Luidens on Presbyterian baby boomers (those born between 1946-1964) also explored those baby boomers who had dropped out of church.[1] The research is helpful in thinking about the dropout phenomenon in several ways, although its focus is on people who dropped out in one denomination and in one age group. The most helpful insight for people in congregations is how the research subdivides the dropouts in terms of where they are *after* their departure. For our purposes I want to focus not on those who dropped back into another church, but on those who are no longer considered "churched."[2]

The research tells us that the dropouts are not a monolithic group. The following differences are pointed out in the research:

> **Unchurched Attenders** are dropouts who attend church six or more times a year without becoming church members. They are uninvolved with church, but may come for the sake of their families. A number of them have misgivings that keep them from church membership. They are more likely than nonchurch members to be involved in stable marriages and to have children. About twenty percent of the unchurched dropouts are in this category.

> **Unchurched Members** represent slightly fewer (about eighteen percent) persons from the dropout sample. These are defined as having a formal membership to a church but as currently inactive. They may attend church from time to time (less than six times a year) and may have dropped out years ago. The research indicates that some of them seem open to being active in the future.

Uninvolved but Religious is the largest category, representing about forty-two percent of the dropouts. This group has no connection or involvement with churches. These people often told the researchers of bad experiences with churches; they were suspicious of religious organizations. They tended to be more relativistic and individualistic, but they consider themselves as having religious concerns and values.

Nonreligious Respondents represented about sixteen percent of the sample. These are people who have given up on religion. Many of them report long-term doubts and youthful rebellions over church; they dropped out between fifteen and twenty. They say they think for themselves on the ultimate questions. The researchers question whether these persons, in spite of having been confirmed, ever made a significant connection with the church.

Congregations concerned about dropouts would do well to look at the different facets of the dropout phenomenon as suggested by this research. Reaching out to these different kinds of people requires varied strategies.

In the final analysis, the most important thing to do in relation to dropouts is to build strong, challenging communities of faith, communities that will stretch and empower congregational members. Where such communities exist, the need to drop out will not be felt.

One thing more. The Hoge-Luidens-Johnson research clearly suggests that many who are out of churches are responding to forces *external* to the churches. Many are not angry or disillusioned, they simply find life outside the church attractive and relatively fulfilling. For them, the *need* for church is not convincing, nor are there as many forces in society encouraging or supporting church membership.

In such a climate one can expect an increasing tendency to what I call "leakage." *Whenever* one crosses a boundary—transferring in or out, even at birth or conversion—there is a greater chance of a member slipping out of the system. A society with great mobility and lowered religious plausibility structures can expect sharply increased dropout rates.

But it is also true that churches that really pay attention to those boundary points may be able to have a significant impact on the dropout rate.

WORSHEET #9

Dropout Ministry

1. Develop a list of those taken off the rolls of the congregation as inactive over the past five years. Find out what you can about them.
   Can you identify which ones fit the research categories? (Every year
   update this with an annual list.)

   a) Unchurched attender (Check visitor list and Sunday school
      and nursery rolls.)

   b) Unchurched member (Check membership list.)

   c) Uninvolved but religious (the biggest group in the research)

   d) Nonreligious

2. Can you identify several with whom exit interviews might be held?
   Are other strategies possible?

3. What areas in parish life seem to generate dropouts? Are there
    actions that can be taken to make changes in the areas?

4. Make a list of parish young people who have graduated from second
   ary school in the past five years. Where are they? Can you do anything to connect them to church? (Every year update with an annual
   list and develop an annual strategy.)

* * * * *

Conclusion

Numbers are not everything, by a long shot. But they are something. The churches ignore them at their peril. In this chapter I have shared a few clues, a perspective, and some homemade tools. In Appendix A, I provide another tool.

A church that does not grow in numbers will die. A church that does not live out active hospitality violates the Church's traditions. A congregation that does not seek its own way to bring the good news to those who do not know it violates a clear directive of our Lord.

NOTES

1. "What Happened to the Youth Who Grew Up in Our Churches," *Congregations: The Alban Journal,* September/October, 1992.

2. The numbers can be confusing here. "Dropout" is a difficult term because some people drop out and then come back; some drop out and go somewhere else; and some drop out and never relate to any church again. In this piece of research young people who had been confirmed in the Presbyterian Church in the fifties and sixties were asked where they were in terms of church membership in the 1989-91 period. Sixty-two percent were members of churches, although at one time or another seventy-five percent of that group had had a period of dropout. Of the total number who were no longer members of the Presbyterian Church, more than half had joined other churches. Slightly less than half were classified as dropouts with no active relationship to a church. What I am talking about here is that half, the ones with no active relationship.

CHAPTER III

Maturational Growth

More Than Numbers

It is heresy to some, but I must say it: MANY CONGREGATIONS
WILL NEVER GROW IN NUMBERS.

Many congregations have been on a decline for years and will go on
declining. There are large and vigorous congregations that will not be
around twenty years from now because of a loss of members. And there
are congregations with dedicated, committed members who will break
their backs to bring in new members, only to see a continuing loss of
membership year after year.

There are whole parts of the country in which church membership is
likely to decline no matter what church leaders do. The western United
States, for example, has significantly lower rates of church membership
than the East or the South. In their research about dropouts Hoge,
Johnson, and Luidens (*Vanishing Boundaries: The Religion of Protestant Baby Boomers*, forthcoming 1993) note that dropping out may be
influenced largely by a lowering of the "structures of plausibility," i.e.,
those social patterns and support structures that affirm and undergird
religious life and institutions. In the American West, the social pressure
of, and support for, religious activity are dramatically lowest. That being
so, we may be seeing in West Coast religious institutional life a foretaste
of what happens when those supports are removed.

If Hoge and his colleagues are right, in areas of the country where
fifty, sixty, or even eighty percent of the population affiliate with a religious congregation now, we may yet see a declining rate of affiliation to
something like the ten, twenty, and thirty percent membership rate found
on the West Coast.

Although we may hope to reverse that trend and work hard against it, it is clear that very large societal forces are at play, forces over which the evangelism committee of a local congregation has limited power. There will be remarkable exceptions to the larger trends (as there are in some megachurches in California and the sun belt today), but most congregations will experience the power of the trends the researchers describe.

There are also whole parts of the country where membership is likely to decline for a completely different reason: The population itself is in decline. Throughout the great plains states, population has been slowly sinking for generations, in some areas for a century. In some towns and cities causes of population decline are more local, e.g., in the rust belt, Appalachian mining areas, towns where a major employer goes bust, or areas where environmental catastrophe occurs. It is just as probable that congregational membership in those areas will match the membership declines in the general population, no matter what church leaders do.

I do not want to make a case for grim necessity or the power of sheer fate. I am well aware that dedicated people can swim against the stream and make extraordinary things happen. There are churches in the most unlikely, depressed, irreligious, declining communities that will, in the providence of God, explode into growth of all kinds. (I remember just such a congregation in the mountain coves of North Alabama, and I know of another over a century ago in the tideland of the East Coast. Both were Episcopal, which ought to prove something about God's ability to overcome resistance!)

The case I am making is that dozens, hundreds, even thousands of congregations have not had that experience of explosive growth, and probably won't; they *may*, but it's not likely. Most pastors now working in congregations and most congregational leaders will live their lives without experiencing any dramatic change in church membership. With a few exceptions, that has always been true of church growth. We celebrate the exceptions (as in some areas of East Africa today, for example), and we should work hard to be such an exception, but the chances are that we will have to work all our life without that experience. If our faith cannot handle that, we are in trouble.

Among the congregational sketches I gave in chapter one, several churches are probably unlikely to grow in numbers. The Church of the

Apostles (page 2) lived and died without much increase in numbers, in spite of doing some important things. Trinity Church (page 5) in the tidelands grows and declines with the birth rate, but the long-term prognosis is down. St. Martin's (page 9) sounds as if it is in a declining community and is likely to share the community's future, in spite of the development of a strong new ministry. It is my guess that the wonderful, faithful people of those fine congregations will never experience a new member class of twenty members!

My point is that numerical growth is important, but that it is not the only kind of growth congregations are called to. Indeed, some congregations who are fated to experience *loss* of members can demonstrate some of those other kinds of growth.

I want to focus here on what Ted Buckle called "maturational growth." It is the ability of a congregation to challenge, support, and encourage each one of its members to grow in the maturity of their faith, to deepen their spiritual roots, and to broaden their religious imaginations. I will give some examples.

The Church of the Apostles was a disaster in terms of numbers, but it did develop a form of religious community that touched a few people at an extraordinary depth. For a few blazing years, these people grappled together with personal dimensions of faith as a small core group. They searched the Scriptures as none of them had before. They tried to make connections between their faith and the life of their community. That was a kind of maturational growth that can be emulated by congregations anywhere, provided some people are willing to make it happen.

Trinity Church, on the other hand, called its maturational growth program by an old-fashioned name—christian education. Miss Marie, who picked it up from her mother eight decades ago, never called it even that; it was "Sunday school" to her. But that familiar name does not describe the power it had in the lives of Trinity's people—students, teachers, and alumni, too. Lives were shaped. Lives were changed. People were connected to roots of faith for life. Her niece's adult education built on Miss Marie's foundation. There are genius-saints like Miss Marie in other congregations. I saw one three weeks ago in a thirty-year-old who has taken charge of education in a suburban congregation. The question for the congregation is how to support this kind of growth when it takes root.

Second Baptist (page 7) faces that question in spades. Caught up in the turmoil of rapid membership growth as the new plant opens, the structures they have that help people grow are threatened with an overload. In the midst of numerical growth that many congregations would love to have, how do Second Baptist's leaders keep on top of it all, developing programs so that both old and new members are helped to grow in faith? A similar problem faces St. Anthony's (page 8). In the turbulence surrounding its ministry to those with AIDS, how does the congregation also care for the growth of its oldtimers? Those who cannot yet see the connection between congregational life and a person with AIDS also have a challenge to grow in understanding. Leaders face the problem of keeping the oldtimers from leaving the parish, but also of taking the positive opportunity for maturational growth, of helping them discover new dimensions of God's healing, caring concern for everyone.

St Martin's Church (page 9) discovered maturational growth in the wilderness of sexual abuse. First the priest, then the people of that congregation discovered growth simply by listening to those in pain. As they listened, they grew in understanding, compassion, and ministry. From listening came forgiveness, then healing, then direction for their ministry.

Those are some of the ways maturational growth is happening in congregations today. But what those congregations are experiencing is part of something much larger, something that requires more systematic thinking and planning.

Congregation as the New Seminary

Early in the 19th century American church people of many denominations realized that they needed to produce an educated group of leaders for the religious life of the new nation. Seminaries were invented to raise up and train a theological elite to lead the congregations and religious institutions. The new invention worked. Through the halls of America's seminaries passed generations of faithful pastors, teachers, and administrators, both for churches and the churches' educational institutions. We called those graduates "ministers," and what they did was what we defined ministry to be. It was a ministry desperately needed in the churches of the new republic. It is still the definition of ministry that most people understand.

But the concept of ministry began to change radically in the middle of the twentieth century (See *The Once and Future Church,* The Alban Institute, Inc. 1991). It is now becoming clear that the ministry called for in the present and the future is not one defined as a professional class of teachers, leaders, and administrators. What is needed is primarily a ministry of lay persons working in the structures of the society. Seminaries were invented for a professional ministry, but it is in congregations that the new forms of ministry are found. For the most part, however, congregations have not understood their task to be the training of the new ministry.

Yet.

That is the issue. The only institution that can produce ministry for the twenty-first century is the congregation. It is the *only* institution that can do for the next century what seminaries have done for the last one—produce ministers. But to do it, they must produce a different kind of minister for a different ministry.

We do not have to start from scratch. For the twenty-first century's ministry we already have a network of congregations. Nevertheless, a formidable challenge lies ahead. One by one, each congregation must be re-invented as a new kind of seminary—a congregation that shapes laity in ministry as effectively as seminaries of the past century shaped a professional clergy.

The analogy to a seminary is important, but it is also dangerous. It is important because it points to how difficult the task is. Seminary founders, faculties, administrators, and funders have worked hard and long to develop the educational processes, the facilities, and the resources to turn out effective pastors and teachers. It took more than a century, and many of our regular seminaries are not yet stable institutions. Building institutions to turn out good clergy has been a hard, time-consuming, expensive job.

Congregations have a comparably big job ahead of them if they are to be the seminaries for a new kind of ministry. It will take time and energy and resources, and it will take people and congregations willing to be pioneers. Reinvention will not be easy.

The analogy is dangerous also because congregations will be tempted to copy what seminaries have done. Already we have congregations training laity using methods and curriculum worked down from "regular" seminaries. The problem is that the new task will require new methods of schooling; a new kind of minister calls for a new kind of seminary.

Congregations must become the primary resources for enlisting, training, and retraining of the ministry of the next generations, but they must develop quite new methods of understanding theology and teaching it. Let me comment on several areas where congregations are called to maturational growth. Because we do not even have the language yet to describe what we need to have and do, let me speak by analogy from what we already know about seminaries.

Basic Curriculum

Congregational leaders today need to plan overall life to provide a full curriculum, not just a few courses from time to time for individual growth. Members of congregations need to be challenged beyond religious dilettantism to serious, long-term engagement with the stuff of the faith. Ministry in the twenty-first century is going to demand persons equipped with the biblical story and with working theologies that translate into working-world realities. Ministers in the marketplace need an operational grasp of ethics that they cannot get in a sermon or two a year. Stewardship needs to get out of the every member pledge campaign and become a working part of how people view the way land is used and environment is managed; they need new perspectives on their careers or their retirements. Not everybody needs everything, and not everybody who needs it is going to want it. But congregations need to begin developing an approach to a full, basic curriculum. Seminaries have a basic curriculum of biblical studies, theology, history, and practical theology. Every student is grounded basically in each area. Congregations must develop a curriculum just as basic for the ministry they are to train for, then tool up to deliver it. Just as seminaries have had to form coalitions for some tasks, congregations may also have to experiment with new, collaborative relationships to mount a full curriculum.

Ministers for tomorrow will not get it if they do not get it in their congregations.

Field Education

Present day seminaries have tried hard to develop a way to use field placement (in nearby congregations, for example) to deepen the training of students, grounding textbooks and seminars in the actual experience of a congregation. In general, seminaries are not able to put many resources into field education. Their resources are severely limited and other, more basic concerns have a higher claim. In congregations, a brand new concept of field education must be at the heart of the curriculum, not at its edges. "Field placements" will be life situations, the everyday job or community responsibility, homemaking or retirement, or the experience of unemployment, or being sick in a hospital. That is where ministry is carried out, and the congregation needs to have a system that helps lay persons reflect on their encounters with God's concerns in that daily work. Congregations must provide times and places in which members can present case material from daily experience and receive help in critically analyzing the theological and missional dimensions of those daily experiences.

While much of what I am saying reflects a critical need to strengthen adult education programs in congregations, the need for field education calls for new kinds of thinking about youth work and children's ministries, too. How can attendance at public school be field education in ministry for our younger members? How do we learn to help them reflect on that as ministry? How will that reshape Sunday School? Youth work?

Faculty

Just as most seminary faculty today get their basic training for their teaching in theological seminaries or graduate schools of divinity, faculty for the new kind of congregational seminary must be trained *in congregations and in working on their ministries in society*. Clergy, trained for one kind of ministry, will not be the best teachers of this new kind of ministry. Let me say it even more harshly: Clergy, by their current training are specifically disqualified for much of the training that must be done in our new congregation-seminaries. Today's seminary dean may be a useful role model for clergy to think about. A good seminary dean today is one who builds up the community of learning, sees that the curriculum is in place, seeks out able faculty, makes sure the fabric is intact, and occasionally teaches a course that is a personal speciality.

Remedial Education

Many seminaries today must have courses on a lower academic level to accommodate students with gaps in their education. Similarly, congregations need to think of "tracks" of training—a basic-training curriculum for beginners and advanced learning opportunities for others. Many who will appear at church over the next generation will come from situations totally apart from religious training, and congregations will need to perceive and respond to the beginner as well as to strengthen the mature. The wide acceptance of Elderhostel education for older persons gives a model for how some segments of the churches could structure opportunities for maturation.

The Theological Education Enterprise

The basic assumption of the seminary enterprise is that the clearest path to theological discovery rises from a deep grounding in traditions of theological scholarship. In the new seminary/congregation, the clearest path to theological discovery rises from engagement with the life of the world, through the ministry of ordinary people. The absolutely central issue is going to be the connection between the contemporary lay person's theological encounter and the traditions of the whole church's heritage. The clergy have a central role in making that connection. It is not a "telling" role as it is primarily understood today, but a "listening" and "connecting" role. I see this as vitally important for clergy, but it is a far different role than they have been trained for or are accustomed to. The primacy of theological leadership shifts to those engaged with the world outside the church; a secondary, supportive, connecting role remains for the professionally trained leader. I am aware that this calls for serious rethinking of how we train our clergy.

One thing is clear to me. Many people and many congregations are already working to get started in this direction. The Church of the Apostles may have been just such an effort. It will take years of trial and error to move from where we are to where we need to be. There will be mistakes and failures. In this area, people need to make haste slowly, and to stay in touch with what others are doing. Impressive curriculum pieces are already being invented, e.g., multi-year biblical studies programs, lay theological education-by-extension programs, and catechumenal systems. What I am pressing for here, however, is not devising some off-the-shelf system for curriculum, but building slowly and steadily toward a comprehensive program that develops by helping each member gain the knowledge, skills, and perspective for a front-line ministry. And that is a life-long program.

WORKSHEET #10

Maturational Growth

1. An inventory of opportunities and gaps in the congregation's "curriculum":

Area of Study	Beginner Track	Advanced Track	Track for Post-Retirement
A. Studies in Literature of Faith			
- Hebrew Scriptures			
- New Testament			
- Contemporary Writing			
- Media			
B. Studies of the People of Faith			
- The Hebrew People			
- The Story of Churches			
- Contemporary Saints and Movements			

(continued)

(WORKSHEET #10 continued)

Area of Study	Beginner Track	Advanced Track	Track for Post-Retirement

C. Faithful Life
    and Ministry

    - Thinking about Faith
      (Theology and Philosophy)
    - Vocation and Faith
    - Morals and Ethics
    - Faith and the Daily News

2. Resources we have or need:

A. How can we develop a group (or groups) to reflect on work and faith on a regular basis. Who can
    help?

B. What kind of ongoing task group can help us monitor and improve maturational growth in the
    congregation?

*****

Maturational Growth in the Spirit

Spiritual maturity or spiritual growth is one of the most elusive subjects one finds around church people. It is clearly different from "education" in the ordinary sense. Some suggest that it is a different order of thing entirely—"formation" as opposed to "education." Seminaries today struggle with what it means and what their responsibility for it is. They wonder how to teach it. There is more confusion about what the seminary teaches in this area than in any other.

Everybody in the church has a stake in spiritual maturity, but few have much sense of what it actually means. Laity, by and large, leave it (like "theology") to the professionals—the clergy and the professors. Any congregation that wants to produce a ministry for the future needs to have a clear picture of what it wants to do in the area of spiritual growth and a program for doing it.[1]

I understand spirituality to involve an open and continuing dialogue between who and what I am with God's intentions and purposes for me. Keeping that conversation going is the issue of my spiritual growth, rather than any particular moment on the way or technique for doing it. Spiritual development is that dialogue. My congregation needs to help me keep it going.

My experience is that the primary enemy of spirituality is stopping the dialogue. It is settling for where we are now into a kind of homeostasis, a "being stuck" in one place, walled in, unresponsive to new possibilities of life. When that happens, the conversation stops. The growth stops.

The rub is that homeostasis seems to be a basic human temptation. Everything in us seeks to get things under control, to make them predictable, manageable. And yet when we get things that way, it all goes dead. Theologians talk about this as our human attempt to justify ourselves, to act in such a way as to be self-justified and in need of no further stretching. Such a life tries to build itself without the necessity for God. "If I really can get it under control, manage my life, who needs God?" Living in that kind of homeostasis walls oneself off from possibilities, not only from grace, but from God as well. Turning away from that self-satisfaction, that ossification of the present, is what repentance is all about. It is in repentance that spiritual growth is born. In nonreligious language, it begins when your socks are blown off by life and you have to find new footwear. Or it can begin in the quiet moment in which you just know that you are being pulled to a new life.

A congregation that helps you with spiritual development is a congregation that helps you avoid getting stuck. That kind of congregation is there in those moments when life explodes in your face, helping you find in the crisis the questions of existence and the call to a new life, as well as helping you get back on your feet. Those are the moments when we are pulled or forced out of safe harbors, when we have to take a new direction.

Sometimes we find in ourselves the strength to move out because we have seen or heard a new possibility for life. The congregation that helps spiritual growth is there, too, in those routine moments that occur in the flow of ordinary life.

Routine Growth

The church's system of pastoral care was built as a system to provide spiritual growth. The system developed over centuries of practice. For routine growth, it provided cycles of Bible readings and celebrations week by week to connect us to different aspects of God's calling to us. The message changes for the time of year and for the different festivals, and the preaching moves through the lectionary. As we go through life, the different pages of our life-script interact with the steady pattern of the congregation's worship and life. In that encounter, we are encouraged forward in the dialogue. All the resources at our disposal presume that our dialogue with God needs to be renewed daily and weekly, and that through that renewal we can turn from the routine toward growth in the Spirit.

There is nothing magic here. This pattern has worked for generations, helping ordinary people grow into God. Indeed, it is so ordinary that we often forget that that is why it is there. The rhythms of Advent and Christmas, Lent and Easter, the commemoration of special times—Reformation Sunday and World Communion Sunday—the annual rally day or homecoming, the spring revival, the vacation Bible school. That's the meat and potatoes the churches have shaped into a pattern to help us grow in the Spirit. For many, it continues to work.

Dramatic Growth

The Church provides different frameworks for the dramatic changes of life—the turning points that almost by definition destroy the homeostasis of life. Birth. Acceptance into maturity. Marriage. Birth of one's own children. Illness. Death. Those developmental earthquakes have shaped lives through thousands of years and still do. They are the framework for another process of spiritual development, the moments when people must face anew the ultimate questions: Who am I? What am I called to be? What do I believe? What must I do? The religious task was to facilitate in those moments a conversation with God, bringing to bear all the wisdom of Scripture and the power of liturgy. We called that pastoral care, and we train people to do it. Its purpose was to facilitate the dialogue between the self and God as the self faced new challenges of life transitions.

Growth through Discipline

Yet a third path to spiritual growth came from giants of the spiritual life who invented ways into the dialogue with God on more continuous bases through meditation and other spiritual disciplines. One of the gifts of our time has been the rediscovery of processes of spiritual direction and spiritual growth derived from spiritual masters and the monastic traditions. Tilden Edwards and Parker Palmer are two explorers and pioneers in those areas, making the resources of this third way more accessible to the rest of us. But little has been done to translate these methods to congregational settings.

Religious congregations have the task of building paths for spiritual pedestrians like me. Their job is to provide frameworks, helps, guides, and resources for the break-out moments that occur, and it is also to help those moments happen. Homeostasis, the state of being stuck, gets interrupted daily for most people, if not more often. Under the pressure of life, we have learned to rebuild our walls and shore up our defenses as fast as we can—just to keep going. We use baling wire and chewing gum to patch together a spiritual homeostasis to get us through. So it is that we come to our worship each week with damaged defenses, looking for but also afraid to find the dialogue that alone can strengthen us for the next steps of life. The role of worship each week is to help us let those defenses down and enter once more into the dialogue that feeds our spirit.

The primary task of the congregation in helping spiritual growth is thus very simple: It is maintaining that steady rhythm of exposure to Scripture and worship week in and week out, year after year. A congregation that allows its worship to become sloppy or routine is copping out on its most central opportunity to provide for the spiritual growth of its members. A pastor who gets caught up in anything else —from pastoral counseling to social action to theological study—and neglects the task of preaching and leadership of worship is in the wrong business.

The secondary task of the congregation is to provide skilled help at life's transition points so that dialogue with God occurs and leads us on. That is a special challenge to us today in our congregations and in the churches. The specialness of the challenge needs discussion.

Individual congregations may or may not be able to provide the specialized help in spiritual growth that comes through sustained spiritual disciplines. But they can surely work, and collaborate, at helping their members find the resources (personal and educational) that can lead them on such paths.

Today's Challenge for Maturation in Spiritual Growth

Modern American life is more complex than the kind of life reflected in the pastoral care systems of the churches. The framework of birth, adulthood, marriage, children, illness, and death is on target. But there is so much more. Each of those moments is a critical change-point, requiring reorientation of life. Each is a potential moment for a renewal of the dialogue with God. The pastoral care system tries to help people actualize each new moment of dialogue as it occurs in life. Where it works, those turning points of life do become turning points in relationship to God. Pastors are trained to be skillful at helping that happen. Many of us have experienced the power of God anew at moments like our own wedding, the baptism of our children, or at the graveside of a friend. Our religious tradition and our pastors helped open up that new moment in our own life dialogue with God. Those ancient traditions and practices really do provide a dependable framework in which the dialogue may move ahead.

What has happened to us in the meantime, however, is that we have discovered that as life has changed from rural to urban, from fourteenth century to twenty-first century, from a life span of four decades to a life span of eight, a lot of changes have occurred in how life crises are faced. Some of the old life crises have changed and new ones have been added.

The traditional framework completely overlooks some big crises that bother us a lot in this modern world, but that were not influential in the times in which our practices were shaped. What the medieval church did as ministry at the time of birth was challenging enough, but today pastoral care requires the competence to minister in moral quandaries about birth control and abortion, prenatal care, premature birth, and birth defects. Similarly the medieval church's pastoral system provided for the move from infancy to adulthood as a relatively uncomplex reality, symbolized in a sacrament of confirmation. Today between infancy and adulthood we distinguish two very complicated categories of life transition that the medieval world did not know about or see fit to include in its pastoral care syllabus—childhood and adolescence. Both are life crises, whether you are going through them yourself or trying to lead your children through them.

The congregation or pastor who helped a bride and groom prepare for spiritual and physical union did not think often or deal with issues of divorce and remarriage, much less birth control and genograms. How a pastor and parishoner faced illness six centuries ago often helped the parishoner encounter a dialogue with God. But Blue Cross? HMOs? Nursing homes? Living wills? Never before in history has the category of "senior citizen" existed in the way it does in this country and century. The opportunities for spiritual growth are ours to discover.

In sum, if congregations today are to help people grow spiritually in the conditions of modern life, they have a larger and much more complex set of life transitions to deal with. Developmental psychology has enlarged our understanding of the complexity of the life changes that most of us will live through. Erik Erickson described eight stages through which he observed people to move. Levinson, Sheehy, and Gilligan built an even more complex set of stages. Pastoral theologians have been slow to respond to the burgeoning need for a broader range of pastoral care that these new understandings uncover. I tell my friends who are pastoral theologians that they should see pastoral theology as the growth industry in theology. We need them to free themselves from fascination with psychotherapy and organization management. There is a large task of spiritual development waiting for better understanding of basic pastoral care.

There are beginnings. Douglas Walrath has given tools for looking at some additional dimensions of this complexity in his book *Frameworks* (New York: Pilgrim Press, 1987). James Fowler has opened some wide doors that connect faith development with life development (*Stages of Faith,* Harper & Row, 1981). Robert Gribbon helpfully synthesizes some of these different schemes of categorizing the crisis points and stages of human life in America in his *Developing Faith in Young Adults* (Washington: The Alban Institute, 1990). Tex Sample's approach (see *U.S. Lifestyles and Mainline Churches* [Louisville: Westminster/John Knox, 1990]) enlarges the scope of pastoral care questions even further.

If there is one thing the churches need today from those in the field of pastoral theology, it is help in working at a new synthesis of pastoral care that does pay attention to modern life and in connecting that synthesis to congregational ministry.

We need help developing tools for maturational growth.

Maturational Growth

1. How can we assess the effectiveness of our regular worship in helping our members in their dialogue with God? Who can help?

2. What opportunities, other than worship, do we provide to engage people routinely in spiritual growth? Who can help?

3. How do we analyze and evaluate what we offer in ministry to those at different stages of life's journey?

Life Issues: Need by those in this stage*	What We Have or Offer in the Congregation	How Effective is It? Rank 1 (low) to 6 (high)

INFANCY:
(1-5)

CHILDHOOD:
(6-11)

ADOLESCENCE
(12-17)

YOUTH
(18-24)

YOUNG ADULT
(25-35)

CAREER ADULT
(36-50)

ADULT
(51-64)

SENIOR ADULT
(65-79)

SENIOR
(80 AND UP)

(continued)

(WORKSHEET #11 continued)

* Note: These categories may need to be varied or elaborated to fit your congregation. One activity that would help in this work would be to list names of those in those age groups, or at least a sampling of the names. Each person you list could give you input for the worksheet.

* * * * *

Conclusion

Numerical growth gets most of the urgent attention and is a concern of every congregation, but it will not be a big part of the experience of many congregations.

For ministry of the twenty-first century, every congregation will need to develop itself into a training ground, capable of equipping each member with a new level of competence in education and formation.

Maturational growth needs to be at the center of the agenda of every congregation's board.

NOTE

1. Back in the early seventies, Parker Palmer, Tilden Edwards, James Simmons, and I carried out what we thought was the first "empirical" study of spiritual growth by going to twenty lay persons and using instrumentation and interviews to discover their spiritual paths. The paper we wrote is long out of print. Soon thereafter Jean Haldane did a similar study of a different population in a paper still available through The Alban Institute: *Religious Pilgrimage* (OD25). U. T. Holmes explored spiritual development among clergy with some empirical testing in his posthumous book *Spirituality for Ministry* (Harper, 1982).

CHAPTER IV

Organic Growth

Understanding Organic Growth

The group of people who eventually became the Church of the Apostles started out with a frustration and a hope. The frustration was that although they were serious about their faith, none of the congregations they had known before either challenged or supported them in ways that helped them grow in the faith. Their hope was that if they could structure a different kind of community, a truly supportive, organic entity, something like an extended family, then each person would have a chance to give and receive as she or he needed.

Organic growth is about the task of building the community, fashioning the organizational structures, developing the practices and processes that result in a dependable, stable network of human relationships in which we can grow and from which we can make a difference.

Organic growth is about interaction between frustration and hope in all congregations. Many people find the structures of their congregation are an obstacle to their ministries, draining energy away rather than generating it to spark mission. Organic growth is the call to shape congregations themselves to become communities that generate life and energy. Organic growth helps the organizational structures of the congregation become a launching pad for ministry, rather than an institutional albatross around the collective neck of the members.

Experimental efforts like the Church of the Apostle's are not isolated; dozens of such communities form every year. Some of them form as "house church" structures within regular congregations. Some, like Apostles, form as a freestanding congregation in their denominations. In the sixties and seventies many of them took on the character of the counter culture. One friend described the beaded, homespun-clad, turtlenecked congregation to me as "post-middle-class hippies." In the eighties and nineties, inspired by the small-group focus of Korean congregations and the South American Catholic "base community" movement, a number of large, "regular" congregations have begun trying to organize themselves into small groups. Chuck Olsen, a Presbyterian pastor and researcher, studied the house church movement from his Project Base Church in the early seventies and noted that such groups tend to have a limited life span (see his *Cultivating Religious Growth Groups*, Westminster, 1984).

These pioneering efforts produce ideas, energy, and significant personal growth, but Olsen learned that it was important that they be related to ordinary congregations that have more long-term stability. His hope was that a strong congregation could spawn house churches, maintain contact, and then be there when the life span of a particular house church came to an end. Conversation between these radical, small-group communities and the regular congregations could be a source of new life and energy. Too often today the ideological commitment of small-group church forms places them in opposition to those in "ordinary congregations."

Apostles succeeded in developing new ways of being an organic community, but it was unable to sustain itself. Of the other congregations described in Chapter I, three others seem to be living with large questions of organic growth. Second Baptist had a strong structural base long before the coming of the new industrial plant changed everything. It had coped well with its place in the community and with its members. Its organic system was adequate. The sudden influx of members—growing almost thirty percent in a very short time—is a threat to its organizational life. Any congregation growing that fast is likely to have much stretching to do. How do the new members get into the decision-making processes? Who chooses and trains the new leaders who are needed? How do you handle the fights that come up over allocation of space or budget? How do you get to know the new people? How does a small community become a large one?

None of these is basically a theological issue; if Second Baptist's numerical growth is not accompanied by organic growth, the congregation will soon be in trouble. Second Baptist has to reorder its life as a community if it is to continue to be an effective base for the religious life and ministry of its members. These are issues of organic growth.

Third Presbyterian, on the other hand, has a very different concern
about organic growth. The pastor and a renewal group have chosen to
make radical changes in the congregation's organic life to reflect their
agenda. Like those who formed the Church of the Apostles, this renewal
group made a commitment to a new kind of life, a congregation that was
organically different, characterized by high commitment and certain
behaviors they value (forms of prayer and praise, ways of disciplining
one another, healing practices, etc). The big difference was that the
people of Apostles *all* made the decision for the new kind of community
so the new beginning was by consensus. At Third Presbyterian, in contrast, a number of people from the congregation decided to change its
character. Other members, who did not choose the new direction and
who felt their congregation had been taken away from them, did not
participate in the change. To them it feels like what Wall Street would
call a "hostile takeover."

The struggle is again in the area of organic growth. The questions
shaping Third Presbyterian are partly about what form of community
best supports ministry and mission. They are also about how to change
the organic life of the community: Is it by majority vote or by inspired
leadership? Are dissidents justified in resisting the efforts of the renewal
group and blocking the change? Is the renewal group justified in forcing
changes on the oldtimers? There are important issues here also about
ownership and power. Who owns this congregation? And if, as some
might well answer, "God," then who has the right to decide what God's
opinion is? Where is legitimate power located in this congregation? In
all of these areas, theological ideas, organizational structure, and personal preferences are mixed together. Healthy organic growth demands
that these issues be explored and teased apart.

Whatever happens, Third Presbyterian is in for some pain. Organic
change of this kind is never simple or easy. Leaders in such a congregation have a responsibility to do a lot of learning about change processes
and conflict management.

Faith Lutheran illustrates the staying power of the organic life of a
congregation. After the excitement and furor around the sudden, temporary influx of university people, the stable structures that had nearly been
overwhelmed by the burst of change came back to the surface. Things
returned to "normal." It is hard to be sure if what has happened is
healthy in the long run. One wonders if they can preserve some of the

good things that came with the upheavel. How can you know when the forces from the past are restoring what is necessary for life and when they are simply restoring an energy-deadening status quo?

Faith Lutheran has lessons for all who want to change a system; the people at both Second Baptist and Third Presbyterian, as well as most of the rest of us, need to go to school on their experience. New pastors need to think a lot about how change really happens.

Those underlying patterns of the organism, the structures that hold things together and support the life of the congregation, do not change easily nor quickly. When you pay no attention to those underlying forces, any change is likely to be cosmetic. The submerged forces and structures will reemerge after the period of change. The once highly visible change will soon fade away.

Organic growth is all about making sure that growth in numbers or maturation or mission is matched by growing a strong and effective organization, able to make decisions and carry them out over time. A congregation cannot accomplish much without paying some attention to its underpinnings as an organism.

Congregations as Social Systems

Every congregation, like every purposeful human group, is more than the sum total of the people in it. This should be no surprise to church people —St. Paul hinted at this when he talked about the powers and principalities that are parts of creation. In our time we put different names to these phenomena as if we had discovered them for ourselves brand new. I like to think that Paul may have had wisdom that far outpaces our ability to analyze and categorize. I must admit, even as I move this discussion in the direction of talking about the congregation as a system, that Paul's language of powers and principalities, demons and angels, sometimes has a truer ring than the organizational language we use to try to communicate some of the same messages. We are talking about things that are mysterious and luminous, but our descriptive language is sometimes mechanical and one-dimensional.

The Congregational Studies Working Group (a talented group of researchers, teachers, and thinkers responsible for such useful tools for those leading congregations as the *Handbook For Congregational*

Studies [Abingdon Press, 1986]), describes four dimensions or levels that one must deal with in understanding congregations:

Program: *What* a congregation does, what appears on its calendar of events and its table of organization;

Process: *How* the congregation does what it does, how decisions are made and leadership is exercised;

Context: *Where* the congregation exists within its world, its community, and the interactions between the two; and

Identity: *Who* the congregation is in its "personality," what its traditions and soul are all about.

Those seeking organic growth in a congregation will find those categories helpful. The *Handbook* provides excellent tools for each level. For purposes of this book, however, I want to lay out another way of looking at congregations as organisms. It is useful, I think, because it gives more starting places, more handles. This language slices the cake in a different way.

Congregations are social systems, i.e., they are complex organisms with distinct parts and orderly processes that somehow form a single entity out of that complexity, within a particular environment. Congregations interact with their environment, receiving resources from it and making contributions to it.

The following simple diagram illustrates the idea of a congregation as a system:

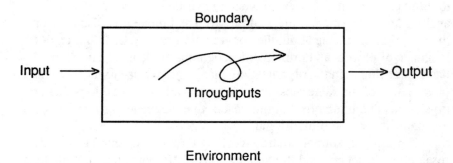

Systems have a boundary that distinguishes and separates them from their environment. They receive inputs from the environment, they act upon those inputs in their own characteristic ways (the throughputs) and they send their outputs back into the environment. A human body is an example of a system. It receives food, water, and oxygen from the environment outside its boundary (skin). Its internal organs process those inputs to maintain the system internally and to exert energy externally. Its outputs, in addition to wastes, include what it does to and in its actions on the environment—running or walking, cutting down a tree, shooting pool, developing a theory, teaching a class, or goofing off. In a social system, large numbers of individual systems combine to interact as a single system. In this sense, a congregation is a social system.

Let's look at a purely imaginary example of a social system. Let's pretend that we own an automobile factory. As long as we are imagining it, let's make it first-class—a Rolls Royce factory! I imagine that this factory is a big building, probably covering several blocks. Everybody who works there is pretty clear that the purpose of this thing is to build Rollses although some of the people, of course, aren't too interested in the cars because they just want to earn a pay check and get home for a ball game on the weekend. Every night I imagine trains backing up to the loading docks, unloading engines and steel and tires and all kinds of things that go into Rolls Royces. Every morning I imagine a whistle blowing and lots of people arriving for work. As they arrive they go off to different places where they know they are supposed to be. Some go to the shop floor, some to cranes or other machines that lift or move the material around. Some go to the paint shop. Some put on jackets that mark them as foremen and others pick up pads and pencils to keep track of things. Others go to the office of the factory where they get involved in checking inventories and making out bills. Some go to meetings to see if there are any changes coming down from company headquarters.

I have one other piece in my imaginary factory. There is a little lean-to down by the factory gate, and one of the workers is stationed there with a little clicker like the ones church ushers use in large churches to count attendance. That worker has a phone connected to the office. When the Rollses start rolling out about mid-day, this worker starts clicking numbers. The people upstairs know there is a target number for the day; when they hit that number, the worker phones upstairs and everybody relaxes. I can imagine the worker one day suddenly discovering

that twice the target number of automobiles came out that day, or perhaps only half as many. When that phone call goes to the office, what a
different reaction! In either case the people in the office would probably
dash down to the floor to see what is going unusually well or badly, and
in the latter case, to try to fix it. If double the number are coming out,
they may also have to phone sales people around the country to see if
they can sell as many as they are producing.

Another diagram:

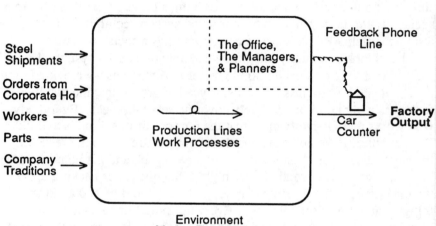

The inputs are all the things going into the factory: The things the trains
bring in the night, the people, the machines and resources, the plans of
the engineers, the company's vision of what it is trying to do, and the fact
that the workers all have a different level of "buy-in" to that vision.

The throughputs are all the things that go on inside the factory: The
different roles and functions of the workers, the way they collaborate and
work together, the way the pieces are delivered to the workers and then
fitted together, the way workers settle differences among themselves or
between groups, and the way everyone has expectations of one another
and patterned ways of doing what is expected of them.

The outputs are the Rolls Royces coming out the other end. Which is
why I put the lean-to by the gate and have the guy with the clicker there.
The function described there is feedback. That worker lets the managers

of the system know if what was intended is being accomplished. (I often wonder, in my imaginary system, what would happen in the office if the worker at the gate phoned up in horror: "We just produced three Hondas!" Of course it couldn't happen; one of the inputs is the tradition of the place as a Rolls Royce factory. That kind of factory doesn't produce Hondas—unless a lot of other things have changed in the meantime in the inputs and the throughputs!)

There is one other dimension. I hinted at it when I mentioned that there might be a need to phone out to find out if sales could handle some extra automobiles. There is an environment out there that this system has to be very sensitive to. If there is a massive shift in buyer attitudes (like those that happened during the oil shortage of 1972), the whole factory could go broke because Rollses were not selling, not because anything inside that factory was being done poorly. The system is dependent upon careful dialogue with its environment.

Congregations are social systems that function in many ways like this imaginary system. Of course the illustration has limitations. It treats a factory producing mechanical goods, not the human and spiritual values we associate with congregations. But I want to press on with my metaphor in the belief that even the flaws in it can help us think more clearly about the organism we are dealing with and provide better guidance in trying to affect them.

On the next page is a congregational system diagrammed in the same way as the automobile factory. I want first to comment on some obvious similarities and differences, raising a question or two, then present some of the elements and processes the two systems have in common. By doing so, I hope to describe some of the leverage points for those who want to engage in organic growth. Please note that systems analysis is usually much more elaborate than this. I am simply pointing to a few of the key elements and processes because they are ones we can most readily affect.

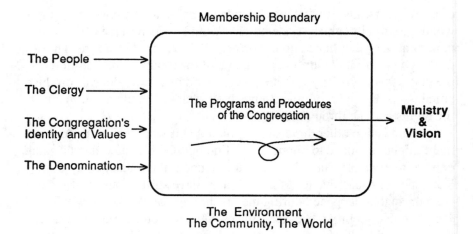

The People ——→

The Clergy ——→

The Congregation's
Identity and Values →

The Denomination ——→

Membership Boundary

The Programs and Procedures
of the Congregation ——→

Ministry
&
Vision

The Environment
The Community, The World

     The congregation, like the factory, has identifiable inputs. Most important are the people—long-time members, newcomers, staff, and even visitors. The congregation has its particular traditions (the Little Traditions) and carries also those of the denomination (the Big Tradition). A general overall vision of what the congregation is in business for is usually part of this tradition. Other inputs include the resources—financial resources, buildings, the books of worship, the scriptures, and the sacraments or ordinances. Finally, there is the organizational system itself, usually some combination of denominational polity and "the way we do things here." They do not come up by train in the night, but they are no less "givens" than anything else brought into the congregation from the outside.

     The throughputs involve the special way the congregation itself works with and uses its resources. Together, the throughputs make up the "specialness" of the life of the congregation. Most congregations of the same denomination use the same hymnal, but how the congregations, the leaders of worship, the musicians, and the choirs interact with the hymnal is absolutely unique in each place. As Rolls Royce factory workers operate in different areas in the factory and in different roles, so do congregations. Characteristically, congregations also try to keep some kind of sensors out there in the environment to see what is going on, denominationally as well as in the community. There is considerable evidence, however, that congregations often ignore their environment far too often. Major changes in the environment occur and the congregation ignores them, only to make desperate attempts to adapt too late.

It is at the "output" end that we run into a snag. Congregations often are so caught up in the process of throughput that they do not get clear about what they are trying to put out at the other end. Here the metaphor can be most misleading, because the output of a congregation is never as definite as a number of automobiles! My point is that without some concern for what the output is intended to be, it is difficult to know how to adjust or change inputs or throughputs to do it better. It is clear, for example, that "getting more members" is an inadequate statement of the purpose of a congregation. More members means more input. Social systems thinking asks the question, "More members for what?" If our congregation has somebody stationed at the gate with a clicker in hand, what do we tell them to "click" for?

WORKSHEET #12

Identification of Outputs

1. What are some of the outputs we want from our congregation?

   a) In the lives of members in their life outside the congregation?

   b) In the neighborhood/community surrounding the congregation?

   c) In the workplaces in which our people work?

   d) In the religious environment (the denomination, the ecumenical community, etc.)

2. What would we look for as evidence that our outputs were on target?

   a) In our members' lives

   b) In the neighborhood/community

   c) In members' workplaces

   d) In the religious environment

3. What evidence do we see that our outputs as a congregation are not what they ought to be?

   a) In our members' lives

   b) In the neighborhood/community

   c) In members' workplaces

   d) In the religious environment

* * * * *

Key Elements and Processes of Congregations As Social Systems

Roles

In the Rolls Royce factory not everybody does the same thing. Some people keep books; some work with metal; some oversee the work of others; and some decide how many cars to make. The clearer the roles are and the better people have been trained in their roles, the more likely it is that the system will work well. People in local congregations also have different roles: the pastor, the treasurer, the head of the board, the head of the education program, the teachers, the ushers. Some of the roles are long-term ones, some relatively short. Some are more central and up front, others are less so. A characteristic problem church people have with roles is assuming that a difference in role suggests a difference in value. Some people seize a role because of its prominence, but do not function well in it. Other people resist taking a role because they do not want to be presumptuous or to take a higher seat, when in fact the system will not work well without somebody competent carrying out the role with authority. Abdication of the power of a role often handicaps congregational systems. People in roles also burn out when they are not supported. When that happens, the whole system loses authority and has a hard time getting its work done. Sometimes organizational analysis and evaluation can assist a congregation in getting clear about roles and seeing that adequate training and support is available for people in those roles.

Norms

In the Rolls Royce factory certain guidelines about behavior were authoritative even though unwritten. These rules were not in the personnel manual or on posters on the wall; they were the behaviors people observed in each other and never talked about at all. They represented a kind of consensus that people had come to recognize as valid for them. In all sound systems, the boundary between what is acceptable and what is unacceptable is enforced by everyone and by no one. Sometimes it is a frown from two or three people when unacceptable language is used.

Or the jokes that go on and on about the shirt that is just a little too loud. Sometimes, system norms also control what people call each other. They tell people where they are supposed to be and when, and what the limits are for being different. Norms generally set limits of behavior around the workplace (you could date somebody who works in the office, but you don't neck in the halls; it is acceptable to argue in meetings, but not to punch your opponent in the nose; people chip in to do their share of the scut work, etc.).

Because these rules are unwritten, they can be confusing to new-comers. A newcomer may violate a norm because nobody thinks to tell him about it. I often say that you don't know what a norm is until you step on it. Thus, a congregation may have a norm that no one ever criticizes anybody or anything. That norm makes it terribly difficult for a congregation to deal with a conflict or even a difference of opinion. A congregation may have a norm that "we are like a family around here," which makes it extremely hard for a newcomer to break in.

Norms can be changed, but it takes work. People at the Rolls Royce plant used to smoke everywhere. Now signs are all over prohibiting smoking. For a while people had to be reminded, but now the signs are no longer needed. A nonsmoking norm has grown up. A congregation can change a norm, too, but it takes much attention and time and rein-forcement. Where a congregation has a norm that members only talk to old friends, rarely will pleading from the pulpit change behavior. Members really have to put in time to figure out how to change that norm, then work at it for a long time. Only then does behavior change. Once the new norm is set, it will be just as hard to change as the previous one and will affect the life of the congregation for years. Newcomers are most aware of a congregation's norms precisely because they are the only ones who have to watch others' behavior so they can regulate their own. Oldtimers don't have to. They already live by the norms, even if they don't realize it. Healthy norms can undergird healthy interactions for years; unhealthy norms can inhibit the organic growth of a congregation.

Rewards and Punishments

We do not like to think of congregations as having rewards and punish-ments, even less that rewards and punishments can affect our effective-ness as a congregation. The Rolls Royce factory has no such problem.

If a person does a good job it shows up in the paycheck or in a promotion. If that same person misses work, refuses to follow orders, or does not produce what is expected, a pink slip is not far away.

Congregations commonly mismanage their volunteer workers by not paying attention to rewards and punishments. This refusal can make the volunteer think that sloppy work is all that is expected. The best management of volunteers is done by holding people accountable, praising and celebrating good work and being prepared to "fire" a volunteer who does not perform what is needed. One of the rewards one can get in working in a congregation is collegiality with the pastor. Yet in many congregations the only people who are rewarded by the pastor's attention are troublemakers, passive-aggressive, or overdependent people. This is not what happens in a Rolls Royce factory. A congregation that wants to grow as an effective organism will try to translate the concept of rewards and punishments so that those strengthening the mission are affirmed and those blocking it are encouraged to change.

Beliefs and Values

Every social system has at its heart a set of values and beliefs that are its center of gravity. When people's deepest beliefs and values get separated from their behavior and the values of system, problems are inevitable. In our imaginary example, Rolls Royce is committed to producing an excellent car, the finest in the world. It will get in trouble if it begins producing cars with slipshod work or if customers begin to think other manufacturers are producing better ones. Church people know this concept in the form of "We must practice what we preach" or "If you're going to talk the talk, you've got to walk the walk." Keeping beliefs and values yoked with behavior is important. But it is also true that it is easy to construct a congregation that simply uses people rather than loving them, where a stranger is ignored, where people are unforgiving and rigid, or where people hide what they find unacceptable rather than bringing it out in the open for healing. A congregation that seeks to grow as a ministering community will work hard to match its behavior to its values and beliefs.

Myths

Most systems analysts ignore this element of systems, but it is extremely important in helping congregations grow in effectiveness. "Myth," as I am using it here, stands for the wonderful, sometimes almost magic stories from the congregation's past that shape the members' understanding of who they are. Rolls Royce managers, I am sure, regale one another with stories about Mr. Royce or the day the first Rolls came out the door. In congregations, the myths are accessible to all. They shape and express basic attitudes and values. The stories may be of "the bazaar that paid off the mortgage," "the time the organ blew up," "the pastor who died in the pulpit," or something else people talk about at the drop of a hat if you ask them to. (Even as I write this I remember a wonderful one: "The day the choir's soprano burst her corset!") The myths are part of the glue that holds the congregation together, celebrating the heroes and heroines of the past and the triumphs and the tragedies that continue to hold power. Some myths also preserve an identity that is no longer true. I remember sitting in a meeting of graying adults who were bemoaning the demise of their vigorous youth program. They saw themselves as "a congregation of young couples with lots of teenagers." It took a while for them to realize that the youngest teenager they had was now a lawyer in the state capital! Myths, like perfume, are meant to be appreciated and inhaled, not analyzed. They are clues to deep meanings and values. Where they reflect unreality, people can be helped to let go of them for better ones. I have learned that one cannot pry people's fingers loose from their myths; they must let go themselves. A congregation that wants to grow needs to be familiar with its myths, constantly seeking to bring them in line with reality, but drawing strength and identity from them, too. Their life as a congregation now will generate myths for the future.

WORKSHEET #13

Elements of Systems

1. Norms:

a) Name behavioral norms that everyone buys into, nobody talks about, and that help us as a congregation to do what we need to get done.

b) Name some norms that everybody seems to accept, nobody talks about, but that we would be a lot better off without.

2. Rewards and Punishments:

a) In what ways do we as a congregation acknowledge people or groups who go beyond the expected and accomplish spectacularly?

b) Name two or three occasions on which some group or committee simply did not perform. How did we deal with it?

c) How could we better recognize excellence?

d) How can we be more honest and helpful where performance falls short?

3. Beliefs and Values:

a) Name three or four beliefs or values we have about how people should be treated.

b) How is our behavior in our congregation in line with those beliefs or in contradiction with them:

1) With church newcomers (give examples)

2) With people from "across the tracks" of our community (whether the "tracks" are socioeconomic, class, educational, ethnic, or whatever). Give specific examples.

(continued)

(WORKSHEET #13 continued)

    c) Name three or four beliefs or values we have about the critical needs of the world that should be addressed by people of faith.

    d) How do we live out those beliefs or values in terms of:

       1) Our worship

       2) Our budget

       3) Allocation of board time? Pastor's time?

4. Myths

    a) What are the great stories about the congregation's past that are told and retold? What is so important about those stories?

    b) Who are the heroes and heroines of the congregation? What was important about them; why do you think they are the ones who are remembered?

    c) What are the stories we tell that are really not in touch with who we are now?

* * * * *

Decision Making

Decision making is the first process of a social system that we will consider after our list of elements. Processes are habitual ways of doing things over time. Decision making is one of those processes.

Exactly what decisions get made in a system is sometimes not as important as how they get made. A Rolls factory or a congregation needs to be sure that there is a dependable, accountable system for making decisions, a system that one can protest and try to change if necessary. The organism needs to build up some confidence that decisions are made in the service of values and beliefs, and that people who need to have a chance to make input get that chance.

There are many ways to make decisions—Robert's *Rules of Order*, consensus, or the dictates of an authority are only three of them. Sometimes a single organization has different decision-making patterns for different kinds of decisions. All of that can be just fine—if people are clear about what patterns operate where. Confusion about how decisions are made makes for anger, poor motivation, and a sense of being victimized. Congregations that want to grow as effective human systems must be very clear about who makes what decisions and how one can make input or protest. It is also important to understand that not everybody needs to be involved in every decision.

Communication

Almost every time we at The Alban Institute are asked to help a congregation, people will tell us that the problem is "communication." Sometimes what they are saying is that they do not like the message or the messenger, not that the communication system is bad! Be that as it may, it is true that congregations often have problematic systems of communication. Formal systems tend to be one-way communication from the parish office to members (mail, Sunday bulletins, newsletters, Sunday morning announcements, etc.). Every parish office knows what happens. People phone to say "Why wasn't I informed" of the meeting that has been in circulars, bulletins, on the notice board, and in the pastor's announcements for the past month. I sometimes wonder if that is why the English have a system of reading the banns for three consecutive weeks to announce weddings.

Rolls Royce factories have found out that some of the shop floor workers are aware of things the managers haven't found out yet. Working at getting two-way communication between workers and managers helps the work go better. Similarly, conversation between work groups who do different things to the automobile often makes both groups work better. A congregation that wants to grow in its mission strength can make a step up in its effectiveness by working to improve the communication system—building in many ways to communicate between groups, as well as to groups, and setting up two-way communication with the office. It is amazing, for example, how much more a congregation hears an announcement when a member of the group concerned, rather than the pastor, makes it.

Socialization

Socialization is the process by which a stranger is brought into a group. Whether we're talking about children or adults, it is one of the critical processes of any social system. Where it is done well, the new member rapidly becomes an effective, contributing member. Where it is not done well, the new member is frustrated, unproductive, and frequently disappears from the group before long. At the factory, workers are carefully taught what is expected of them—what the hours are, who their bosses are, who to go to if they are having trouble, how to use their tools, when they will be paid, what uniform is required. In the beginning they may even have someone who leads them through the system formally, step by step. By the time this training is over, the factory has a worker who knows what to do and when to do it. The better the system works, the more satisfied the worker is. Factories have learned that it is very costly to have to replace dissatisfied workers every few weeks. Such workers not only cost in time and reduced efficiency, they also become people who hate the company and "bad mouth" it in the community.

Congregations, by contrast, have paid little attention to socialization. We are told that half the new members who join a congregation disappear within two years. From a strict systems point of view, that is terribly costly. What gifts those people brought and wanted to contribute are now cut off, and the congregation is the poorer for it. Second, those people are very likely to tell their friends what a lousy place that congregation is. But beyond a systems point of view, the congregation has also violated its own beliefs and values. They have failed to receive and give hospitality to one of God's children who was seeking to make a home in the community.

Congregations cannot spend too much time developing ways to help the newcomer find her or his way into community. This is not an organizational issue alone; it is also a basic issue of the faith. I am pleased to hear of more and more congregations putting energy into what we at Alban call New Member Ministries. Socialization does not happen without paying attention, planning processes, and ensuring that skilled people are at our many gates.

The socialization process is broader, however, than what happens just for the newcomer. Rolls Royce has a training program for the workman who gets promoted to foreman. Congregations need to recognize that every time a person moves into a new role in the congregation, they need training in the new position. And every socialization process—whether into membership, a guild, or a role on the board—is an opportunity for the congregation to communicate its deepest meanings and values once more. My work with church boards has made me aware that very few congregations pay any attention to training board members for their new role; that lack of attention has messed up a lot of church boards. It is also responsible for the burn out and disappointment of many wonderful people who agreed to serve.

Boundary Maintenance

One process that seems vital in human systems is the process of maintaining clarity about the boundary of the system—what is inside and what is outside. It is not difficult to see the value of this for our hypothetical factory—you do not want an untrained person off the street messing around with expensive equipment; you do not want a Ford salesman to see prematurely the plans for next year's model; you do not want a person working at a local service station enrolled in the company's pension system. A congregation that cares about its effectiveness needs also to look to boundary maintenance.

Boundary maintenance means identifying the distinguishing characteristics or behaviors that constitute membership. For many congregations boundaries are very loose indeed. Anybody whose name was somehow placed on the mailing list is thought of as a member. For another congregation one is not a member unless one undergoes a careful, three-year training program and agrees to tithe and attend every Sunday. I do not argue here for any particular definition of membership, but that a congregation grows in effectiveness if it pays attention to the issue of its boundary. Most mainline congregations have paid very little attention to boundary issues, assuming a very open and inclusive membership. This can communicate openness and inclusivity, but it can also communicate that it doesn't matter very much whether you belong or not. Many congregations wake up to this issue, discovering that they have several boundaries operating—one for "congregational friends," one for "high holiday" members, one for "regular visitors," one for "pledgers," one for "regulars," etc. There are several issues to work on in boundary maintenance: what membership means, what different categories of membership might be, how one gets in and is trained for membership, how the system deals with those who do not live up to membership standards, and how to deal with those who leave.

One of our major learnings has been the importance of boundaries *when they are crossed.* Two are obvious—the boundary of entry into the congregation and the boundary of leaving. Chapter II noted possible ways to improve a congregation's ministry at these key moments, with the focus on the person being ministered to.

The point in bringing up boundaries here is what they mean to the life of the community. The external actions, especially those associated with worship, welcoming new persons, or saying goodbye to others, lift up the whole life of the community and the importance of one's commitment and participation.

A second point is the opportunity for positive training in membership every time one crosses a boundary. At such points the congregation's values, norms, and history can be rehearsed not only for the benefit of the new member, but also for the reinforcement of the wider congregation. It is clear from my experience that practices such as tithing begin to be influential when they become part of the training of those crossing a boundary onto the board or the boundary of membership classes.

Work on boundaries can help strengthen the organism of the congregation in many ways.

Our example congregations have a number of boundary issues. Second Baptist Church, experiencing a strong influx of new members, is facing a threat and an opportunity at its boundary. If it works hard to train the new members as they enter, it will reinforce those directions and values that the congregation stands for even while it forces itself to clarify those directions and values. If it pays no attention to what has been important at Second Baptist in the past, that distinctiveness is likely to be lost in a few years. The opportunity for numerical growth is also an opportunity for organic growth.

At Third Presbyterian the issue is the meaning of the boundary of membership. There are two definitions, two boundaries. The renewal-based new leadership has a sharp definition that excludes even some who have been members for years. The older membership group understands the boundary as more inclusive, in line with how they understand the church. How this conflict is settled will sharply influence the organic nature of the congregation. What happens to the organism will be fought out on its definition of its boundary.

Leadership Development

Leadership development refers to the way roles of power and authority are distributed in a system and how persons in those roles are trained for them. In many congregations many of those roles are defined in books of order or church law, but the more important definitions are established by the interaction of people and passed down informally from one gene-ration of leaders to another. Even the well-defined roles are modified, sometimes beyond recognition, by this rich heritage of personal interaction.

In every congregation in which I have worked, a key leadership issue has been how the ordained leader understood and acted out her or his role in relationship to how the lay leaders understood and practiced their roles. At Faith Lutheran Church, a talented young pastor radically changed many aspects of a congregation's life, apparently without engaging congregational leaders in what she was doing. Now that she has left, congregational life is returning to what it had been before she came. This points to the power of pastoral leadership to make interventions, but the necessity of engagement with long-time leaders if lasting change is to occur.

The question of leadership always involves the dynamic first described in Douglas McGregor's historic article and book, *The Human*

Side of Enterprise (1947). To what extent is leadership authoritative and to what extent participative?

Each lay leader and each ordained leader comes to the relationship with presuppositions about what "ought" to be the right relationship. Rarely do those expectations coincide. Rarely do those expectations even get discussed. One gets a hint of a cultural difference in understanding ordained leadership in the story of Third Presbyterian. Renewal leaders in this case expect the pastor to act out of an authoritative model that violates traditional members' understanding of how Presbyterian polity works.

Some of The Alban Institute's earliest research (see Roy Oswald's *The Pastor as Newcomer,* The Alban Institute, 1977) describes the difficulty that occurs when a congregation shifts from a very authoritative pastor to a very participative one or vice versa. Patterns of relationship take a long time to change; a "different style" pastor, even when specifically requested and wanted by congregation leaders may find that old patterns hold sway for years after a change is made. This can be very frustrating.

Conflicts that may seem explosive often develop from a mismatch of expectations. Often consultative intervention may be required to help sort out the angers when that happens. Very often such help can cause a dramatic breakthrough unless one or the other of the parties is too rigid to modify their expectations or behavior.

Although we are clear that leadership development as a process of social systems requires attention to both clergy and lay leadership roles and to the dialogue between the two, the churches focus most of their energy at one point: the education or training of clergy.

Most of the clergy training—in seminary or in continuing education—is of limited help in terms of the issues of leadership development I am describing here. Although each clergy person needs to increase her or his cognitive skills and tools in many fields (theology, biblical studies, liturgy, history, etc.), an increase in those skills does not help in leading a congregation as dramatically as an increase in some behavioral skills— basic human relations and communications, conflict management, negotiation, team building, etc. There are all too few opportunities available for clergy to learn those skills.

For twenty years my colleague Roy Oswald has specialized in helping clergy strengthen these experiential skills in a field we call Clergy

Development. Speed Leas' leadership in conflict management training for clergy is also widely known. Educational programs have been developed by Lead Consultants, Inc., and clergy also find help through some new Doctor of Ministry programs such as the one pioneered by Bob Worley at McCormick Seminary in Chicago.

One troublesome fact in leadership development is the virtual demise of basic human relations training for clergy since the heyday of the sixties and seventies. A few continuing education programs (Virginia Theological Seminary in Alexandria and Princeton Seminary in New Jersey among them) provide some components of that training for a few clergy. The training institutions (e.g., Mid-Atlantic Training Center, the New England Training Institute, Consultant Trainers of the Southwest) have fallen victim to declining budgets.

Strategic Intervention Points for Organic Growth

Our experience is that organic growth in congregations is episodic. It occurs mostly at special times and not uniformly through history. It may be analogous to the experience of individual maturation Eric Erickson describes as periods of latency followed by periods of growth.

Paying attention to those special moments when growth is more likely will help congregations and their leaders focus energy at change-points. There are many growth opportunities uniquely experienced by particular congregations, but I want to note six specific points at which growth is unusually possible. These are also points at which outside energy (from a consultant, from the denomination, etc.) is most likely to be effective.

1) *The Change of Pastors*

Every congregation changes pastors from time to time. This moment is predictably critical for change.[1] When one pastor leaves and another comes, there is an unparalleled opportunity for growth in any congregation. It is a time when all of the elements and processes of the congregation as a social system are up for reexamination. This is a time to explore norms, what the congregation affirms and denies, and what its deepest values are; it is a time to revisit congregational myths, heroes, and heroines. It is a time to rethink how choices are made at the point of the most important decision the congregation will make for years. It is also a time to review how communication happens and to improve it. It can be a time to rediscover who is in this congregation and how they want to be involved in its new life. It is an unparalleled time to think about how new members—and the new pastor—can be oriented to what is special about the congregation. To see the change of pastors as merely a matter of administrative juggling of available personnel, or simply as a job to be filled, is to miss out on a great opportunity for growth in a congregation. That is why I call it an event of congregational development, not an act of clergy placement. It is, in fact, both, but it is preeminently an opportunity for congregational growth.

Faith Lutheran Church shows the critical impact of pastoral change as a congregation, but it also shows what may happen if the clergy placement issue takes priority over the congregational development moment.

The Methodist cabinet sending a new pastor to St. Andrew's Methodist Church saw the strategic importance of pastor placement. It remains to be seen what the impact will be on the congregation and the community.

2) *Pastoral Installation and Start-up*

The early months and years of a pastor's work in a new situation provide another key moment for helping a congregation in its organic growth. At Alban, we find that everybody understands, in those early months, that some adjustments need to be made. Generally people are not angry or bitter about how the expectations of the pastor and the congregation have inevitably been just a bit off-base. They are not angry or bitter yet. But if left alone, many of those early disappointments can turn to bitterness and anger. Sometimes congregations and pastors can do this renegotiation by themselves, but we find that using a wise coach or third party consultant works very well here. The consultant can help identify the points with potential for difficulty, and help congregation and pastor make the incremental adjustments that can lead to years of productive work. Although this moment is usually overlooked as a moment of organic growth, we have found it to be one of the best.

3) *Church Fights*

More than any other person I know, my colleague Speed Leas has been responsible for helping congregations discover that the trauma of a church fight is much more than trauma. Each fight has the potential to be terribly, desperately painful; some of them can even be tragic. But in almost every case, a fight can also open a door to growth.

To go into a church fight is often to enter a system where the hidden dynamics have become pathological. Communication patterns have broken down. Leadership has become separated from people. Beliefs and values have become weapons. Boundaries of every kind are invoked or transformed into formidable barriers. Even though many church fights are pathological, and we are all too often called in after the pathology has nearly killed the patient, there often remains enough energy and concern to build a healthy community. I sometimes think that a fight can be a cry of desperation by a congregation to rediscover its own health, to cleanse and rebuild itself so it can bring ministry and mission to people and to a community. The intensity of the fight is a sign of the positive commitment members have to their congregation.

Because church fights can be very difficult to understand and manage, we have come to realize that this moment of opportunity is a moment when congregations often need skilled outside help. One of Speed Leas' most helpful insights has been that church fights errupt at very different levels of intensity. He describes the differences between fights that are (1) problems to solve; (2) disagreements; (3) contests; (4) fight-flights; and (5) intractable conflicts. (*Moving Your Church Through Conflict*, The Alban Institute, 1985). A helpful chart of these concepts was published by the Presbyterian Church (USA) as its *Conflict Intensity Chart V* (that chart is available from the Publications Office, Presbyterian Church (USA), 100 Witherspoon, Louisville, KY, 40202). Because we believe conflict to be an intervention point for growth, and not just a painful experience to get through and forget as fast as possible, we at The Alban Institute have ourselves developed and encouraged others to develop resources dealing with this scary moment in congregational life—publications for laity and clergy; training in conflict management for executives, clergy, and laity; as well as training and deployment of specialists in consulting with severely conflicted congregations. Church fights are painful, but they are also moments that can be seized as opportunities toward health and strength.

Of our illustrative congregations I suspect that two are on the edge
of fairly serious church fights—Third Presbyterian and St. Anthony's
Catholic. Outside help now might turn the pain of conflict into growth
pain. *Might*, I said. There are no guarantees.

4) *Planning*

From time to time congregations go through some type of planning
exercise. Dozens of planning outlines are available and most are useful.
Even planning guides developed for other kinds of organizations can be
adapted for use in a congregation. Some are a bit better than others, but
not so much so that one need spend a year or two looking for exactly the
right one.

All planning is an adaptation of a basic rational framework; scien-
tists call it the scientific method. It consists of a series of steps; different
planners number and subdivide the steps differently and propose different ways of organizing to do it, but essentially they are the same. First,
there is a decision to plan, then a study that tries to clarify where things
are in the planning agency and its environment. Alternative directions
are then generated and analyzed, a direction is proposed and chosen, and
the organization gears up and does what has been proposed. In the after-
math, the agency evaluates how well the plan worked.

Many planning manuals make an enormously complicated process
out of all of this, but it is not necessary to do that. What I call "demy-
thologized planning" is what my wife and I do when we have guests for
dinner. We think about who they are and what we have in the refrigera-
tor. We think about what they might like and recall what we served the
last time they came. We then draw up a list of options, check out what's
on special at the grocery store, and make a decision. We rhwn split up
the work, buy the food, and fix it. Then we have an evening with our
friends. Afterwards, we sit up and talk about what went right and what
we'll change next time they come over. That's planning. You can do a
lot more if you want to, but it's best to fit the planning to the situation.

With congregations it can be that simple or it can be quite complex.
But simple or complex, the potential for growth, for working out the hidden dynamics of congregational systems and developing them along with
the plan, always exists. Although the planning may be triggered, for
example, by a need for Sunday school space, it can give the opportunity

to find out what is going on in the community environment. Is the community undergoing a spurt of growth? Does Sunday school growth mean that other dimensions of the congregation need rethinking? Is there an impact on church music or finances? Who are the people coming into the community? How do these people get invited in and how do we treat them when they come? How is our leadership system holding up? Who will make what decisions and how? Planning a building, potentially, is seeking to grow a stronger, healthier congregation as well as solve the problem of too few Sunday school rooms. It is that "as well as" that I press for.

Second Baptist is the one among our illustrative congregations that simply *has* to get some kind of planning going. Its organic structure is being overwhelmed by the demands of numerical growth and program growth.

5) *A Project*

Congregations have no trouble finding projects to do. Denominations, too, have projects to promote in congregations. Regional judicatories (conferences, dioceses, presbyteries) come out almost annually with "this year's project." Program developers could quit today and every congregation would have projects galore until the eschaton. Pick one or two a year if you want people to keep busy.

On the other hand, I would plead for a different orientation. Look at one project—any project—in terms of how it can help.

Some congregations need to try some very simple, easy projects to build the confidence that they can do something. Some congregations need a project that can give them a sense of accomplishment, particularly after a failure. Some congregations need a project that helps them simply be together after a bad fight. Others need a project to help build a relationship with a new pastor. Some need to be done because they provide a way to train new leaders. Iin short, projects need to be taken on or not taken on to help the congregation grow where it needs to as an organism, a functioning community. The subject matter of the project may be almost irrelevant when viewed from this perspective of growth. The subject of the project may, however, have *great* importance in terms of other kinds of growth in the congregation.

Almost any project can be an opportunity for organic growth.

Stony Valley Church, thanks to its small endowment, seems to have "found" a project that focuses a lot of its life in Detroit. It is interesting that they seem to have found it as a result of a planning effort. St. Martin's Church on the other hand seems to have almost stumbled into its project. Both of these illustrate how a project can strengthen the organism, yet both also point to the next chapter on incarnational growth since the specific projects carry the congregation's values out to the community.

Worship

The worship of a congregation is such a given of its life that one frequently overlooks its central role in the congregation's growth as an organism. Recognizing the enormous variety in styles and focus for worship, we must also realize that worship is where a congregation acts out what it most understands itself to be. Worship is *the* activity that is at the center of the congregation's life week after week. It is the one place where the people in a church fight have to meet, where the deepest beliefs and values are affirmed and repeated, where leadership and roles are most clearly defined, where a newcomer sees acted out what it means to belong to this congregation, and where old-time members act out what the congregation means for them. It is also the one place where the experience and story of the past meet the hopes of the future. In the worship of a congregation the possibility of growth touches members more deeply than at any other time or in any other activity in which the congregation takes part. What happens in worship is the most important thing about that congregation. Whoever seeks to help a congregation grow would do well to encourage them to move deeper into their own traditions of worship.

Conclusion: Organic Growth

I have described many dimensions of the growth of congregations as effective human communities and organizational systems. In all of this I am attempting to put language to and suggest tools for dealing with the congregations that were passed down to us from former generations and within which we live now.

Understanding congregations as systems gives some mental images to use in working with what we experience in congregations. To be able to recognize and analyze roles and norms, to reflect on rewards and punishments, to identify beliefs and values—all give us new handles for dealing with and strengthening congregations. To see the dynamics of defining and maintaining a boundary, to be able to think about how people *became* members of the congregation and its groups, to be able to make judgments about what to do in different kinds of conflicts, and to see the distinct tasks of leadership development, all give us new opportunities to be change-agents as well as caretakers of our congregations. To be able to think *strategically* about points of intervention frees us to be wiser than we were, more open to striking while the iron is hot to encourage organic growth.

Some congregations will have opportunities for numerical growth: all congregations are impelled to seek numerical growth. All congregations must provide for the maturational growth of members; some will be able to excel. All congregations have potential for organic growth; those who neglect their potential will undercut their ability to sustain growth in any other arena.

NOTE

1. See *Critical Moment,* The Alban Institute, Washington, DC, 1986.

CHAPTER V

Incarnational Growth

Outposts of Ministry

In our model of growth that is "More than Numbers," we have talked about three of Ted Buckle's four kinds of growth. We discussed the important point of numerical growth first, then we explored growth in maturity of faith, describing how congregations can help that happen. Then we looked at how congregations are also called to grow as living organisms, systems, and human communities.

This chapter brings us back to a question we began to approach in the last chapter: What are the "outputs" of a congregation's ministry? What is it that a congregation seeks to export from its life back into the life of the world, the social environment in which it exists? Ted Buckle, in describing the fourfold concept of growth he saw in Auckland, assumed that the output would be an enfleshment of the principles and faith of the congregation in the stuctures of the community.

In this chapter we will discover that it may be more complicated than that if we listen to what some modern research tells us. We will explore what some of the options are for a congregation that wants its faith to make a difference in its world, and we will look at what it looks like for a congregation to take seriously what Ted Buckle calls "incarnational growth."

Different Views on Relationships with the Environment

Over the past few decades many people have pondered how a congregation can and should make an impact on the world around it.[1] Two major research projects have been attempted, each of which throws light on the subject.

The Church and Community Project of the Center for Church and Community Ministries, led by Carl Dudley, worked with forty congregations in the midwest over a period of several years to discover how ordinary congregations actually got involved in social ministries within their communities. In the course of those studies, Dudley and his colleagues discovered that congregations had quite different understandings of how they were called to relate to their communities. They found that congregations were distinct from others in the same denomination, as well as from others in the same community. The question "How do you think your congregation should go about instilling its values or concerns in your community?" would produce almost as many answers as there were congregations asked. Nevertheless, nine patterns emerged from the study.[2]

In the second major research effort, David Roozen, William McKinney, and Jackson Carroll studied the relationships between 413 congregations and community in Hartford, Connecticut. They reported some of their findings in *Varieties of Religious Presence*.[3]

The Hartford research helps us understand why it is often difficult to be clear about how a congregation wants to be related to its community. The researchers discovered two variables in how congregations were oriented theologically—"this-worldly" and "other-worldly." Within each of those theological orientations was also a distinction between those who focused on their own membership and those who focused on persons outside the congregation and were pro-active outside the congregation. The researchers diagrammed the differences as I have in the figure on the following page:

	Member-Centered	Publicly Proactive
This-Worldly Orientation	1 - CIVIC	2 - ACTIVIST
Other-Worldly Orientation	3 - SANCTUARY	4 - EVANGELISTIC

The **civic orientation** describes a group of congregations in which there is great sensitivity to the life of the community and a sense of the congregation's responsibility for public life. Civic congregations tend to be supportive of the orderly processes of government and systems of law. At times members of civic congregations will be active or even vocal in political campaigns, working for or against particular candidates or issues. When they do, they operate as private individuals. Pastors and other leaders in such civic congregations will encourage members and young people to take an active part in the political process. In system terms, civic congregations seek to produce members who as responsible participants in society are active in shaping a community that cares for human needs. Among our illustrative congregations, Trinity Church in Virginia and First Church in Middletown exemplify civic churches.

The **activist orientation** describes congregations that sometimes operate as a counter culture, seeking redress of wrongs, protesting public policies that its members consider unjust. Members of an activist congregation—with or without their pastor—may sometimes be involved in public demonstrations about their concern. Whereas the civic congregation tends to support the structures of society, the activist congregation tends to be suspicious and confrontational toward those structures. (Although experience of the sixties and seventies called attention to congregations of this orientation, America has a long tradition of such congregations dating from the time of abolition and temperance and reaching into more recent concerns of civil rights and poverty, the rights of women, and pro- or anti-choice issues.) Such congregations, in terms of the questions of this chapter, would be interested in changing laws and community practices. They are interested in producing members and groups skilled at community change. In system terms, their outputs would be movements for social justice, a community with a higher consciousness of justice issues, and people committed to prophetic life in the community. The Church of the Apostles in Tennessee was an activist church.

The **sanctuary orientation** describes a very different family of congregations. The focus in this kind of congregation is on developing a relationship with God in this world that will carry over into a triumphant life after death, where the trials and tribulations of this present time will be overcome. The outside community is not the focus of change efforts; it is seen as a dangerous but necessary testing place from which to return to the congregation for restoration and renewal. In system terms, the congregation with a sanctuary orientation is not interested in outputs that influence society; it is interested in producing people of faith who can stand against the powers of the world and finally attain to everlasting glory. These congregations seek to produce saints for glory, not a changed society. This is a very different idea of output. None of the congregations in my illustrations is a sanctuary church by this definition.

The **evangelistic orientation,** like the sanctuary orientation, is primarily concerned about the world beyond this one. It differs, however, in that it does understand a very powerful calling to relate to those outside the congregation to win them to faith. These congregations may share with sanctuary congregations a real suspicion of society, seeing it as a dangerous place of personal testing. But those members also see a calling to witness to their faith and thereby to win outsiders to faith. With an ultimate focus on an output of saints for glory, like the sanctuary orientation, the evangelistic orientation is also characterized by an aggressive output of energy into the environment to recruit members. Its secondary output, therefore, is a highly visible community effort to increase the size of the community of the faithful and to enhance its character as sustainer and up-builder of the faithful for warfare in the world.

Third Presbyterian in Seattle has a leadership cadre interested in

changing what had been a "civic" church into an "evangelistic" church.
Such cultural change usually generates fireworks. The case of St.
Andrew's Methodist Church may involve a similar attempt, although it
is too early to know for sure.

These four families describe something of the diversity of how congregations see their relationship to the world, but we should also remember that these descriptions are artificial constructs. No one congregation
fully fits any of the descriptions, and every congregation probably has
people or groups who share a quite different orientation from that which
predominates in the congregation. In using these terms —evangelistic
and sanctuary—it is a good idea to remember that they are specific to
this research and to the Roozen, McKinney, and Carroll book. The terms
"evangelistic" and "sanctuary" have other meanings in other contexts.

It is clear that there are quite different ways to articulate what a
congregation is trying to do or produce in its community. We must use
care and allow for these important differences when we try to help a
congregation grow in its ability to actualize its faith in its community.

Three of the church stories in chapter one indicate limits of the
research categories. St. Anthony's, St. Martin's, and Stony Valley
Church look like relatively conventional civic congregations of their
denomination. St. Anthony's has a special ethnic slant, St. Martin's is
rural, and Stony Valley's location in a changing city has challenged its
civic church pattern. But each has been pulled into relationship with the
community by a ministry need that they discovered in the environment.
St. Anthony's got pulled into AIDS ministry without planning and in-
tentionality, simply because some people got involved. Some church
members are having trouble with the ministry, but is it because they
worry that their church is being taken over by these "activists" or is it
because AIDS itself is so frightening? St Martin's similarly had a community ministry thrust upon it by responding to pastoral needs.

Stony Valley, on the other hand, intentionally set out to make a
difference for the people of the community. It operated through classic
civic church patterns of committees and planning. A church committee
is asked to do a study about how to allocate some funds; it studies the
community and reports back. The report is accepted and a program begins to help people find jobs. Again, a civic church begins a very active
role in the community.

The uniqueness of the struggle between what each congregation sees itself to be and what it feels it is called to do clearly means that each will enflesh its ministry in the world in an unique way. That is what incarnational growth is all about.

Because my assumption in writing this book is that it is important for congregations to be concerned about how they enflesh their values and concerns in the environment around them, I want to speak primarily to the three categories above that have a concern for and focus on the life of society and how to change it—*civic*, *activist*, and *evangelistic*. Congregations of each of those types are vulnerable to particular temptations. These temptations are explored next.

The Christendom Temptation

Wanting to make a difference in the community, seeking incarnational growth, leads church people into the heart of the revolutionary change occurring around us in the world. But today it also leads us into temptation.

Most Christians today inherit a worldview of "Christendom" as a set of unquestioned assumptions about how world and church ought to be related. I say we "inherit" this world view in the sense that that world view shaped the institutions of the churches we have—their systems of order, their patterns of power distribution, even their educational institutions, seminaries, and systems of finance (See *The Once and Future Church*, The Alban Institute, 1992, for my fuller argument).

In other words, we are waking up in a world in which a previous set of assumptions about the church and the world are clearly wrong and are crumbling around us. Yet those assumptions were the framework of the world we knew last night when we went to bed. And we cannot be sure what parts of our remembered mental furniture still have substance this morning.

Can you imagine going to sleep in a familiar room in a familiar neighborhood that you've known and loved all your life and awaking in a room that's dark and moving around?

We should not be surprised that it is here in the Church's relationship to the world around it that the Church is most tempted to reconstruct the old empire. Our remembered history, our instincts, our institutional patterns, and our own fear of the unknown combine to pull us continually back from our pilgrim journey to rebuilding the empire we left. Here more than in most places we yearn for the fleshpots of Egypt and are tempted to turn back from the promise of God.

When we begin to talk about how we want a congregation to make an impact upon society, we run directly into what I call the Christendom Temptation. We try to take the church today and use it to rebuild Christendom. We become caught in an attempt to reconstitute a marriage of church and state so that they interpenetrate one another. We seek an oligarchy of religious and political leaders to call the shots for society. We look for a coalition of "the right people" to establish a new consensus in which the church sets the moral agenda. The proposed coalitions of political and religious leaders to enforce a view about abortion or homosexuality is the Christendom Temptation. The call to make America "a Christian nation" is the Christendom Temptation.

We should not be surprised. There are biblical examples of similar temptations. It is like being taken up the highest pinnacle of the World Trade Center and shown the empires of the world. Are we not tempted to want the power to shape them all? It is the temptation to equate our own vision of Church and society with the Kingdom of God. To name it is to expose it as a fraud. Such an empire never existed and never will; yet it remains true that the *dream* of such a possibility lies behind much of history and has been the energy that has driven men and women to make a difference.

Let me describe three ways I see us tempted toward the Christendom paradigm, each somewhat analogous to one of the types described from the Roozen, McKinney, and Carroll research.

The Temptation to Construct a Just Society

An activist congregation is often tempted to build a Christendom version of the Just Society. It assumes that a political order can be constructed that incarnates fully the principles of justice. The attractiveness of the temptation is obvious. Religious people of all sorts in Western society have always longed for a society that incorporates personal caring and justice, that protects the poor, that brings the strength of the strong to assist the weak. Most of the major biblical figures call for such a society.

A clue to the empire-building nature of this temptation is the role of clergy in it. Generally clergy are the leading figures, the prophets *and* movement heads, even when they send their followers into the battle they have pitched. This is a temptation of Church to take authority over Empire. The laudable aims of the activists become the pressure for empire building in a new way.

The temptation creates a two-fold problem. It assumes that the religious people have a corner on knowing what that justice looks like; it also assumes that the power to enforce such a society can be administered and organized coherently and justly. Take one example of the problem. What is "justice" on abortion? Most of the people I know are clear about the answer to the question. The problem is their answers do not agree. More than that, the most passionate on whatever side have what I can only call contempt or outrage for those on the other side. And many of the people who are most articulate on both sides have deep religious convictions they call upon to support their position.

Religious people who care about the state of society have a hard time not projecting their passion onto God, seeking to build a society that enforces their own convictions about what is true and good. When they do, they often become the antithesis of their faith—hard, unforgiving, rigid, monomaniacal, intolerant.

I am not saying that religious people should not be seeking to work for justice in society. I am simply saying that 2,000 years have left us with a legacy of wanting to legislate the whole thing in our own image. We leave no room for pluriformity.

Religious congregations need to be developing prophetic voices and nurturing prophets. They need to be very careful when they begin writing a prophetic agenda for the state.

The Temptation to Rebuild a Religious-Secular Coalition

The civic congregation in the Roozen-McKinney-Carroll typology is tempted to rebuild an "establishment" of the right people and institutions and groups, closely in touch with one another, quietly consulting about critical issues of the day. Each has its own realm of power, but there is such an interpenetration of values and concerns that a basic consensus among power brokers emerges. In this coalition statesmen consult with bishops and moderators at prayer breakfasts before undertaking great enterprises of war or peace. Civic religion reigns.

The enticement of this view is that most of us can think back to a time when such an establishment seemed to work. There's the rub. "Most" of us. In fact, such coalitions are always blind to the large segments of society that are left out in the cold, excluded from participation, unnoticed in suffering. Yet "most" *did* see and today remember that more orderly, simpler life. Even those victimized and excluded by the establishment sometimes are tempted to a return to simple—but at least predictable—victimization!

Denominational executives get tempted in this direction by flattering invitations to lunch and a conference at the mayor's office or the governor's mansion.

Much of what is called "outreach" in local congregations tries to make a difference to those who suffer and it is profoundly right in this motivation. The temptation I am describing creeps in to turn it into a religious public welfare program. The temptation leads congregations to make outreach to the oppressed the primary task rather than an expression of a community whose primary task has to do with relationship to God. Yes, the two are related. But congregations *must* be grounded in relationship to God and yet have very limited capacity or expertise to accomplish the other. Most such efforts carve out a small arena in which a congregation is tempted to assume it is about the task of rebuilding Christendom. Congregations are not very good at that, and they run into problems of burning out staff and volunteers.

The Temptation to Make A Universal Holy Club

Evangelistic congregations, as defined by Roozen, McKinney, and Carroll, are pulled in another direction toward rebuilding Christendom. Their pull is to build a religious community for all people, parallel to the social and political realms, but without much interaction with society, except on the levels of personal piety and morality. Political rhetoric about family values is code language for this.

The concept is rich in many ways. It builds on yearnings for community and meaning that everyone feels. It builds also on the nineteenth century's passion for world mission and the dream that all mankind will be united in faith.

The problems are obvious. There is no evidence that the fragmentation of religous bodies is decreasing. The stronger the sense of the church as a holy club, the greater the temptation to devalue the outsider or to wall oneself off from the outsider.

All my signals point to a world of increasing complexity and pluriformity. The temptation to a Christendom empire of a holy club is a movement to build an exclusive empire disengaged from important parts of God's world.

Basic Ingredients of Incarnational Growth Today

Although I am disappointed by many efforts of the churches to get their message into society, the imperative to do so remains a part of the charter of the churches. Each of the kinds of efforts noted above seeks engagement with the world differently. The more they can resist the temptation to universalize their approach and avoid the temptations toward Christendom, the more they will learn about incarnational growth.

The simple stories of real churches, and how they went about trying to make a difference wherever they ran into pain and hurt, tell us how ordinary it is for congregations to do this. Each does it in its own special way.

Paradoxically, even those efforts that may go too far in trying to resurrect an old world view may yet move persons and groups toward bringing the faith into dialogue with the world. A lay couple may cook dinner for a homeless shelter mainly because their pastor insisted that they not let the Methodist Church down, but yet the hungry are fed and compassion is expressed. The bishop may go to lobby the governor for a hopeless cause, yet the governor is reminded that there are imperatives and values larger than his desk.

As my son has told me, quoting Chesterton, "Anything worth doing is worth doing badly." Reluctantly, I agree. I do not believe any effort is truly lost, and I am not sure that God is as focused on motives as we are.

I see two basic directions for congregations who seek incarnational growth: Building and Sending.

Building

Congregations must build themselves up as religious communities, as bases from which ministry is done. They need first to get clear that this is their primary business. They are in business to help people find God

and be found by God, to build a community in which God's Word is
studied and reflected upon, a community in which people are nurtured,
healed, and fed.

If this is indeed primary, congregations have a hard task in times of
institutional decline like now. They must become ruthless in cutting
away what is secondary and tertiary. If they have more than enough
resources to cover their first priority, they should move to helping others
join them in that first task before going on to the secondary and tertiary
priorities of their own. Why? Because there is no second team. No
other institution in society has that primary task or will become that
religious community if congregations do not. Radical commitment to the
congregation as an institution is therefore central—not to the present
form in which any congregation now exists, but to the congregation that
God calls each congegation to become.

Sending

The second task is sending. The flesh through which the values and
meanings of the Gospels will make impact in the social order is the flesh
of people who are nurtured in congregations. Theirs are the feet and
hands and brains that will grapple with the ambiguities of the world,
making successful and unsuccessful attempts to make a difference.
Often they will not know the difference between their successful and
their unsuccessful efforts. Nobody will.

The better a congregation gets at building up its base as a religious
community and sending its people to engage the world, the more it will
generate incarnational growth.

Building and Sending Together

The two are not separable, but they are different. They are reciprocal.
Good building of religious community ends with good sending; good
sending demands return and restoration in community.

Bruce Reed of the Grubb Institute speaks of this dynamic relationship as the process of oscillation between a state of dependence upon
God in the nurturing community and a state of committed energy in the
world of work and engagement (*The Task of the Church and the Role of*

Its Members, The Alban Institute, 1975). Betty O'Connor describes the dynamic as the journey inward and the journey outward. The experience of the churches is clear: building and sending do not exist without each other.

If there is a danger to the church's incarnational growth, it is that we have been unwilling to put in the energy to build up the religious community that alone can *ground* incarnational growth. The church of the late twentieth century is in danger of focusing so hard on sending and outreach that it neglects to restore and repair the community which alone has the power to restore and send.

Growth of any kind begins with the congregation.

NOTES

1. This enterprise is quite distinct from the equally interesting and perhaps better known work of those who have been exploring how "church" relates to "society" or "culture." Preeminent among those efforts have been two classic books—H. Richard Niebuhr's *Christ and Culture* and Avery Dulles' *Models of the Church*. Despite the profundity of insight in each of those books, neither deals with congregations at all. They deal with the idea of church and the idea of culture. The work we are talking about focuses on that church there on the corner and the town in which it exists.

2. Dudley's work has been reported in a number of articles, in the project's newsletter *Church and Community Forum*, available from CCCM, 5600 S. Woodlawn, Chicago, IL 60637, and in his book *Basic Steps Toward Community Ministry*, The Alban Institute, Washington, DC, 1991.

3. Pilgrim Press, 1984. A summary of part of this research was published by Alban as *Religion's Public Presence*, by the same authors.

CHAPTER VI

Growing Your Church

Your congregation is important. That is the conviction with which I begin and end my work. Your congregation needs to grow and can grow. This book is an argument for as wide as possible a definition of growth and a real appreciation of the importance of many kinds of growth. It also assumes that not everybody is called to the same path.

Right now, every congregation is pressured and threatened. There are the obvious economic threats, but there are threats even closer to hand than the annual budget. The secular if not antireligious mindset of media and social institutions make it difficult for us to communicate our faith easily to others, even our own children. The institutions of our society seem to make larger and larger claims on our time and energy.

What is more, the anti-institutionalism of our society has infected us, too, and we are reluctant to commit our energy to working on an institution. Our own loss of belief in institutions cripples our ability to engage in the hard work of growth. We are part of the problem.

The central importance of the congregation is its corporate, institutional nature. That corporateness is the prime medium for its work. It is one of the few places in society where we as individuals can come together, restore our wholeness, recover our sense of direction, receive the power to do what we must do, and be assured of the community with God and one another that makes life worth living. The sense of a community that truly is a body of many parts is as central to us today as it was in the first century. It is, however, harder for us today to believe in that body.

The congregation is the arena for the restoration of life and mission. That arena itself needs repair and restoration very critically at this moment in history.

As we saw in the stories in Chapter I, congregations everywhere are in various stages of change. Some are dying, some are being reborn. Some are moving along in very traditional patterns, and others are experimenting with new paths. Some are marking time, perhaps waiting for death. Most of these stories are not terribly dramatic, except perhaps to the people living them out, and that is drama enough. The story of your congregation is probably no more dramatic than any of these.

Because congregations are changing, they need care, attention, wisdom, and leadership through this time. Church leaders who want their congregations to grow are likely to get more results for their efforts at such times of change.

I hope many congregations are going to discover growth in the number of committed people brought into their life. Although I recognize that most congregations will not experience dramatic numerical growth, I look eagerly for some that will–that, one by one, they will bring new persons to new life in community. I also look for congregations to learn to minister effectively and strongly where there is no such growth, or even where there are losses. Their tasks may be more difficult, but are no less a part of the mandate to grow.

The next generation in the churches must do pioneering work in maturational growth. New methods must be invented and old ones rediscovered. A whole generation, nurtured largely in a secular world and living in a nonreligious set of institutions, will need formation and education into the life of faith and its implications in society.

In the near future we must engage church leaders and pastors in the greatest task of discovery and invention of two millennia—a reinvention of the institutional framework of faith. The congregations and judicatories we now have are already being called to become new. That call is partly heard in the increasing collapse of what no longer carries meaning. Leaders and pastors, infected with society's distrust of institutions, will need to take a leap of faith to give the energy and massive resources necessary for the reinvention of the church itself. That is the daunting task of organic growth.

In every community, the congregations of people of faith will also be called on to respond to human and community needs. The responsiveness has always been there, but in the times ahead there will be a need to learn new ways of collaborating in ministry. The corporate and political forces we have counted on in the past may be less helpful in the future.

Each congregation is called on very simply to become more of what God calls it to be. Each one will have its own path. I have laid out four ways that congregations grow and I have described some tools for working at growth. I do not believe that all congregations can grow simultaneously in all these ways, but I hope some can. A congregation that makes a disaster of one kind of growth may experience another kind, and it may even come back several years later and succeed when it had failed before. I believe, in short, that congregations can develop and grow in many ways.

I began with the stories of some ordinary congregations. I told their stories as I knew them because each, in its own way, is trying to be what it understands God to be asking it to be. We can all see that the stories, even the story of the Church of the Apostles whose doors closed years ago, *all* the stories are unfinished. Each congregation has seen growth of many kinds. We have hints that many other kinds of personal growth may lie behind the public stories.

Each of the congregations is unique. The path to growth in each congregation is unique. Each of those stories is unique. The next story is yours.

A Growth Grid Study Framework

Introduction

This Growth Grid Process is offered as a way for leadership groups (either the board, vestry, consistory, session, or a larger group of leaders) in a single congregation to get an overview of how their congregation is doing in the four areas of growth described in this book.

This process is not for planning or program analysis, it is simply to help the congregation begin to identify where it has strengths and where it is less than strong. It can lead to some choices for action or it may serve only as a diagnostic tool.

It is to generate discussion and elicit different people's experience.

Because each of the four grids can generate a fair amount of conversation, it is best not to use them all at one sitting. If they are used at regular monthly meetings, it would probably be best to assign one chapter and do the grid associated with it at each of four meetings. At a retreat, the four could be spaced through a day with time for breaks.

To enhance interaction among participants, and even to generate different opinions, we suggest putting the grids up on a blackboard or newsprint, with the discussion leader listing contributions in the appropriate boxes.

When the four grids are complete, it may be obvious where task forces need to be appointed either to begin some planning or to gather further data.

If you do decide to begin planning some response to what is learned here, remember that sometimes the best place to start is where you already have some strengths and have experienced some success. Starting with the most difficult issues may lead to premature burn out. Don't start on the issue that makes you feel guiltiest! Start where you think you can make a difference and also have some fun.

Be very modest in what you decide to do. Not all congregations are called to grow in all areas at once. Try to pick one or two spots in which you have confidence that something worthwhile could be developed.

All of this work is participating in building ministry. And, the way you work together is also ministry. You don't have to get it all done before ministry starts. Take your time. Start modestly. Start slowly. Start where you have energy. But start!

Growth Grid I

Numerical Growth

Describe the strengths and weaknesses of our program and ministry in these areas:

<u>**Strengths**</u>   <u>**Weaknesses**</u>

1) Recruiting new members from people moving to town or unchurched otherwise

2) Assimilating new members into the congregation, making space for them and helping them fit in

3) Training new members in our values about membership

4) Helping members reevaluate and renew their membership from time to time

5) Keeping track of members who go away to school or on temporary assignments

6) Keeping track of members who reduce church attendance or pledges

7) Helping members connect elsewhere when they leave

8) Other

Growth Grid II

Maturational Growth

Describe the strengths and weaknesses of our program in these areas:

	<u>Strengths</u>	<u>Weaknesses</u>

1) Education or nurture programs

    a) Nursery and Preschool

    b) Children

    c) Youth

    d) Young Adult

    e) Adult

    f) Seniors

2) Special areas

    a) Spiritual direction and/or retreats

    b) Serious biblical and theological
      study

3) Emergency/crisis ministry and aftercare

4) Life-crisis ministries

5) Quality of week-to-week worship and preaching

Growth Grid III

Organic Growth

Describe the strengths and weaknesses of our organizational structures in these areas:

<u>**Strengths**</u>   <u>**Weaknesses**</u>

1) Effectiveness of leadership

    a) In planning and decision making

    b) In managing conflicts

    c) In setting and carrying out priorities

    d) In handling mistakes

    e) Managing finances

2) On ability to recruit, train, and nurture broad leadership

3) The quality of our life as a community

4) Opportunities to know one another on personal level

5) Other

Growth Grid IV

Incarnational Growth

Describe the strengths and weaknesses of our program and ministry in these areas:

<u>Strengths</u>   <u>Weaknesses</u>

1) Our formal outreach activities to
    homeless, hurting people

2) How are our members related to
    community agencies of care?

3) What is our relationship to groups
    advocating change in the
    community?

4) Opportunities to discuss commu-
    nity, national, or world issues in
    light of our faith

5) Opportunities to work with others
    on implications of faith in work
    situations

6) Our opportunities in worship to
    pray about community issues
    and concerns

7) Our awareness of what other
    members do at work

8) Other